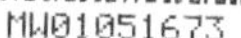

Disney Bento

BY MASAMI MIYAZAKI

CONTENTS

Character Bento

Themed Bento Box Recipes

Silhouette Bento

For Special Events!

HOW TO USE THIS BOOK

- One tablespoon is 15 ml, 1 teaspoon is 5 ml.
- A 600-watt microwave was used in this recipe book.
- Most character details that you'll make out of nori are glued on with regular mayonnaise. If you will need something else instead, we'll mention it in the recipe.
- All vegetables, such as carrots or broccoli, should be boiled in salted water before adding to each recipe. For tiny vegetable pieces, boil 10–30 seconds. For large vegetable pieces, such as broccoli florets and carrot slices, boil 1–2 minutes.

BENTO 101 TOOLS

The tools you'll need to create these recipes should be easily purchased at any standard kitchen supply store, or you might have them already!

Straw

You'll use straws to punch the eyes and nose of the characters out of the nori sheets. The straw on the top right is an extra-wide bubble tea straw (14 mm/0.55 inch); the straw on the bottom left is an extra-thin straw (2 mm/0.08 inch) that came with a baby beverage carton. Having a couple of different sizes of straws will make it easier for you to create the different sized facial expressions of the characters. You can punch out circles and ovals (by squeezing the straw) and teardrop shapes (by flattening one side of the straw).

Milk carton, baking paper, permanent marker

Use milk cartons to create your templates (p. 8). You can also use baking paper for templates, but it tends to bend or crinkle more easily than a standard milk carton.

Use baking paper to cut the shapes out of the nori sheet. You can draw directly on the baking paper with permanent marker.

Scissors

A small pair of scissors with thin blades is recommended for cutting the nori sheets and the imitation crab. Craft scissors are fine too, but make sure to use a brand-new pair, which you will only use to cut food.

Cling wrap

Use cling wrap to shape the rice and create the characters. It will also help keep your workstation and your hands clean and tidy.

Tweezers

Use tweezers to hold the nori pieces when gluing or adjusting the characters. For handling delicate parts, using tweezers is much easier than using your fingers.

Toothpick

The cheese slices are soft, so you can easily cut them by tracing over them with a toothpick (p. 8).

Nori sheet puncher

Just one push and you can punch shapes out of the nori sheets. There are various shapes and expressions, so prepare them according to the character you want to create. If you are going to use a craft puncher, make sure it is sterile.

Garnishing knife

A small knife with a sharp tip is helpful when cutting out small, detailed shapes. A garnishing knife usually has a baller on the other end, which you can use to carve round shapes out of fruits and vegetables.

Round piping tip

Use these to punch out character parts from vegetables, thin omelette sheets, cheese, etc. They come in various sizes and it can be useful to have more than one. Use the thin tip to punch out small circles and the large end to punch out large circles.

Cutter

If you already have Mickey or Minnie or other character-shaped cutters, you can create your bento much faster. You can also use star and heart cutters on vegetables and cheese.

INGREDIENTS

Here are the ingredients that are often used in this recipe book and are useful for character bento.

The recipes in this book ask for two types of peas. When we reference **snow peas**, we are referring to the shorter, flatter type of peas in a pod. When we refer to **snap peas,** we mean the rounder, thicker pea pods. The recipes in this book use peas in their pods, so there is no need to remove them.

Rice

We use short-grain rice for the recipes in this book because it's sticky and easy to mold into the shape of characters. You can mix the rice with rice seasonings and ketchup to change the color of the rice. Molding the rice while it's still warm will help it to retain the shape you want.

Nori sheets

Nori is used for the eyes, eyebrows, and eyelashes of the characters. Taking out your nori sheets in advance and letting them warm to room temperature before working with them can soften the sheets and make them easier to cut.

Snow peas

Snow peas are often used to create the eyes of the characters. Boil the snow peas in their pods in salted water and remove the strings along with the peas inside before use.

Cheese

Cheese is also a convenient ingredient in making character bento. You can use a slice of any type of white cheese (right) or cheddar cheese (left) to make the skin of the characters.

Bread

Use a piece of bread as the base of the character in the bento. You can also create characters out of bread.

Carrots

With their natural bright orange color, carrots are often used for the nose of characters or as decoration. Don't forget to boil the carrots in salted water first.

It's not always easy to get **fresh quail eggs**. They can be found online or at Asian supermarkets and farmers markets. Some supermarkets also have canned or pickled quail eggs, but since the bento is made for children, please check the flavor before putting them into a bento box. In this book, quail eggs are mostly used for decoration. Using mozzarella balls or small rice balls may be easier. Each recipe includes specific guidelines for ingredient replacement.

Chikuwa

Chikuwa is fish cake (surimi) that has been steamed or broiled after being wrapped around a stick. It ends up looking like a tube. *Chikuwa* means "bamboo ring," which is what it resembles.

Eggs

Create thin omelette sheets to use as the character's face and hair. You can change a sheet's color by adjusting the amount of white and egg yolk as well as by adding brown sugar and ketchup to it (p. 9).
A quail egg can be boiled and cut into a certain shape with a cutter or be dyed yellow in a curry liquid mixture.

Sliced meat

Ham is often used as the skin or base of the characters. You'll use ham (top left), salami (top right), and chicken or turkey breast (middle) most often while making bento.

Sausages

Sausages are often used as side dishes to fill the gaps in bento, and they're also used to make certain parts of the characters. You can use sausages, frankfurters, and little smokies to create different shapes and colors.

Kamaboko fish cake

The red outer layer of imitation crab is perfect for red parts such as the mouth or clothes. To create large red areas, you can spread the outer layer out flat. You can use multiple pieces if necessary.

Use the fish cake for white parts. Adjust the thickness of the fish cake by cutting off the excess parts.

Deep-fried pasta

Used when attaching the character's ears (p. 8) as well as ingredients that tend to move around easily. Pasta will absorb the moisture of the ingredient and soften by the time you eat it, so you can often use it without frying it, but if you intend to eat the bento right away or attach bread to it, you should use deep-fried pasta.

Mayonnaise/honey

Ingredients that will fall off easily should be glued down with mayonnaise. You can also use honey if you are gluing things like bread or other ingredients that go well with a sweet flavor.

CHARACTER CREATION TECHNIQUES

These are the techniques that are often used in this recipe book.
We will also teach you some little tricks to make your final bento look even nicer.

CUT

Paper pattern template

You'll need to trace out some shapes for most recipes. You can find the proper shapes on the internet and print them out or trace them from the book. Place the stencil on top of the milk carton and trace the outline with a marker. Use scissors to cut along the marker line on the milk carton and make sure that the marker ink is cut off and will not get on the food.

Ham, cheese

For cutting ham, place the milk carton stencil on top and use a garnishing knife to cut around the contour.

With cheese, you can use a toothpick to cut around the stencil and use a straw to punch out circle or oval shapes.

Nori

Place the baking paper on top

When creating parts such as the eyes and mouth of a character, trace the shape of that part on baking paper with a permanent marker. Place the baking paper on top of the nori sheet, hold the paper and nori firmly in place, and cut the shape out with a pair of scissors.

When you want to create several nori pieces of the same shape, hold several layers of nori and cut them together to save some time.

Using the nori sheet puncher

Place the nori sheet in the slot and push down on the button. You can quickly create nice-looking patterns and facial expressions.

ATTACH

Some of the smaller parts of a character, such as the ears, are difficult to attach to the main parts. In this case, you can use pasta sticks to hold them together. If the ingredient is too hard to poke a pasta stick into, first use a toothpick to make a hole.

GLUE

Pick up the nori and ham pieces with the tweezers to put a little mayonnaise or honey on them. The mayonnaise or honey will work like a glue and attach the parts.

HOW TO MAKE THIN OMELETTE SHEETS

Thin omelette sheets are a must-have to create character bento.
You can change the color of an omelette sheet by adjusting the amount of white and egg yolk, as well as by adding brown sugar and ketchup to it.
We will show you how to make a smooth, bubble-free omelette sheet.

Basic thin omelette sheet

INGREDIENTS

Egg	1 egg
Sugar	¼ teaspoon
Potato starch* or cornstarch	a pinch
Vegetable oil	a dash

*Potato starch, or *katakuriko*, can be difficult to find outside of Japan. You can substitute regular cornstarch if katakuriko is unavailable.

1

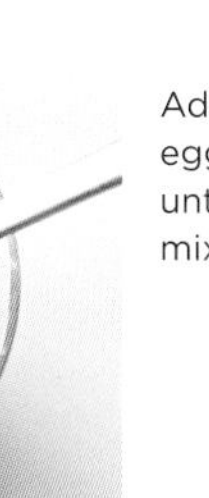

Add sugar and starch to the egg and whisk it with a fork until the white and yolk are mixed completely.

2

Pour **1** through a tea strainer.

3

Cover the surface of **2** with cling wrap to remove the air bubbles.

4

Grease the omelette pan with vegetable oil and heat it over low heat. Pour **3** into the pan and make sure the egg mixture is evenly spread out. Once the edges of the egg start to harden, place the lid on, turn the heat off, and steam the egg with the remaining heat.

There's a mild color difference between the two sides of the omelette sheet. When creating the characters, please show the side that doesn't touch the pan.

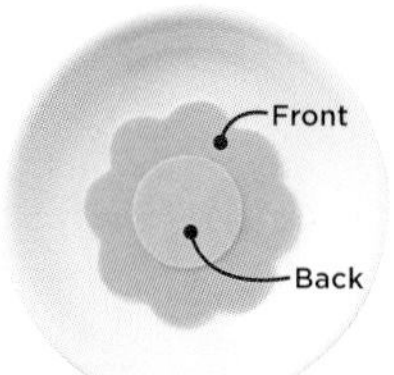

Basic colors
Used for these characters:
Donald Duck (p. 16)
Daisy Duck (p. 17)
Winnie the Pooh (p. 22)
Jessie (p. 41)

Less yolk (more white)
Used for this character:
Elsa (p. 26)

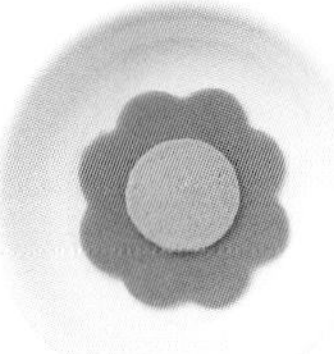

With ketchup
Used for these characters:
Nemo (p. 33)
Dusty (p. 35)

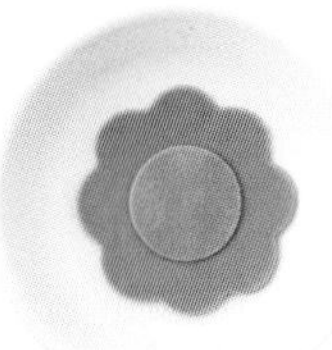

With brown sugar
Used for this character:
Anna (p. 27)

BASIC BENTO TIPS & TRICKS

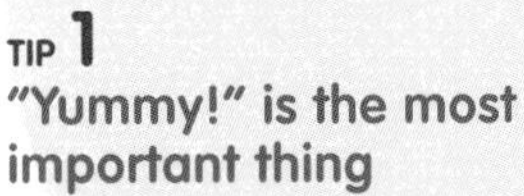

TIP 1
"Yummy!" is the most important thing

Being able to say, "It looks yummy! I want to eat it! It *is* yummy!" is an important part of the bento process. Though in this book we focus more on the design and details of the characters, when packing your bento, please take the taste and color of the side dishes into consideration as well. Avoid using ingredients with too strong a flavor or too much food coloring. Instead, make the best of the color and texture of natural ingredients.

TIP 2
Make it easier to eat

When preparing bento for children who are still learning how to use utensils, cutting bento foods into bite-size pieces can be helpful.

TIP 3
Provide the right amount of food

Make sure you pack the right amount of food in children's bento so that the kids won't get overfull or become hungry again too quickly. Having the right size bento box can help you manage the amount of food packed in each bento meal.

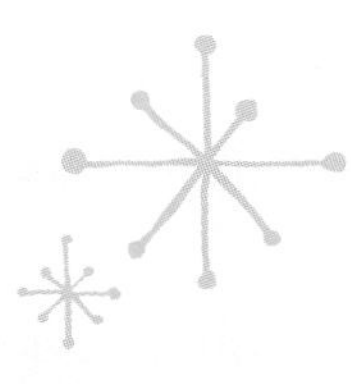

TIP 4
Make it colorful

It is said that a bento with well-balanced red, yellow, and green colors is also nutritionally balanced. Also, a colorful bento is fun and appetizing, so we advise you to think about the colors of the bento when choosing the side dishes. When the colors seem a bit plain, you can always add extra color with food cups, bento grass, and decorations.

TIP 5
Remember food safety

Moisture makes food spoil quickly. To prevent a moist bento, pack foods only after they are completely cooled down and all the extra sauce in side dishes are removed. Most importantly, always fully cook everything going into a bento.

HOW TO PACK A BENTO

1 Start with rice or bread

When you are packing a bento, always start with the rice or bread so it can be a base for the characters that you will add later. Determine the amount of rice or bread you will include based on the space needed for the side dishes and vegetables that you plan to put in as well.

2 Pack the main dishes

Place main dishes in a muffin cup or parchment paper to prevent the flavor of sauce from getting on other dishes, especially when you have dishes that are coated with ketchup or mayonnaise.

3 Pack the side dishes

Fill in the open areas with side dishes. Arrange them nicely so that the bento looks colorful and balanced.

4 Pack the vegetables and fruits

Pack the bento box fully to prevent the character and food from being tossed around during transport. Fill in open areas with vegetables and fruits, but always keep in mind the balance of colors. You can also use bento grass, wax paper, or other dividers to separate fruits so they won't absorb flavors from the other dishes.

5 Add the ears and hands

Place the delicate parts of characters at the end so that they don't get messed up during the packing process. This will make it easier to pack the side dishes too.

Cute! CHARACTER BENTO

MICKEY MOUSE & FRIENDS

Mickey Mouse

Look at that smile!

BENTO MENU

- Japanese meatloaf ▸p.89
- Chikuwa fish cake flower ▸p.91
- Bacon-wrapped french fries ▸p.92
- Mickey's hand (a layer of ham and cheese made with a Mickey's hand cutter and decorated with nori)
- Snap peas, cherry tomato, lettuce

INGREDIENTS

- Rice .... 3.5 oz./100 g
- Nori sheet .... as needed
- Chicken breast or turkey breast .... 1 slice
- Cheese slice .... a small amount

RECIPE

Paper Pattern Template p. 43

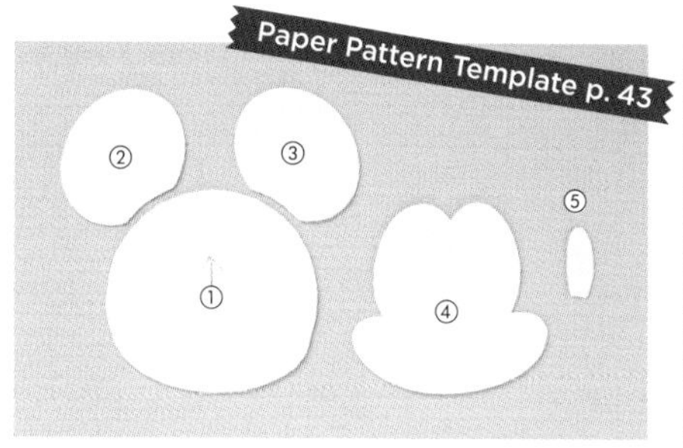

1 Create the paper pattern templates out of a milk carton (① Head, ② Right Ear, ③ Left Ear, ④ Face, ⑤ Eyes).

2 Separate rice into three portions: one 2.1 oz./60 g and two 0.7 oz./20 g. Mold these three portions into the shape of paper templates ①, ②, and ③.

3 Place a sheet of nori on the surface of the head rice ball and wrap it with cling wrap.

4 Wrap the ears with nori sheets too and leave them for 2–3 minutes until the nori turn soft and cling to the rice balls.

5 

Once the nori on the rice balls has become soft, place them into the bento box along with the side dishes and vegetables.

6 Cut the chicken or turkey breast along the contour of paper template ④.

7 

Place the chicken or turkey breast from **6** onto the head rice ball.

8 

Cut the cheese slice along paper pattern template ⑤ to create two eyes.

9 Place the cheese from **8** onto the face from **7**. (Flip one eye over to use as the other eye.)

10 

Trace the shape of the mouth, the eyes, and the line under the eyes on baking paper and use these to cut the nori.

11 

Place some mayonnaise on the back of the nori pieces from **10** and glue them onto the face.

ATTENTION! Look at the illustrations of the characters to see how you can adjust their expressions!

MICKEY MOUSE & FRIENDS **A cute wink!**

Minnie Mouse

RECIPE

Paper Pattern Template p. 43

1 Create the paper pattern templates out of a milk carton (① Outline, ② Leftover Outline of Face Cutting, ③ Face, ④ Left Eye, ⑤ Ribbon, ⑥ Center of the Ribbon).

2 Pack ⅔ of the bento box with rice and fill in the open area with side dishes and vegetables. Place paper template ① on top of the rice and cover the rice around it with Japanese scrambled egg.

3 

Place paper template ② on top of the scrambled egg and fill the open area in the center with seasoned ground meat.

4 Cover the seasoned ground meat from **3** with cling wrap and gently press it with your hand to flatten the surface.

5 **ATTENTION!** Hide the deep-fried pasta in places that will be covered by the eyes, nose, and other facial features.

Place paper pattern ③ on the cheese slice and use a toothpick to cut around it. Place the cheese slice on top of the seasoned ground meat and secure the cheese with a deep-fried pasta.

6 Place paper pattern ④ on the fish cake and cut around it. Cut the shape out of the fish cake and place it onto the face.

7 Trace the shape of the eyes, the eyelashes, the line under the eye, the nose, and the mouth on a piece of baking paper. Place it over a nori sheet to cut the shapes out and glue them onto the face.

8 Place paper patterns ⑤ and ⑥ on the soft salami and cut around it. Cut the shape out of the soft salami and attach it onto the top of the head using deep-fried pasta.

BENTO MENU

- Swordfish sautéed with ketchup ▸p.90
- Simmered tri-color veggies ▸p.93
- Cheese sandwiched in a cherry tomato, flowers made from carrots and snow peas, broccoli, lettuce, rice

INGREDIENTS

Japanese scrambled egg (mix eggs with sake, sugar, and powdered dashi and scramble in a pan until flaky) ······ as needed

Seasoned ground meat (add soy sauce, sake, sugar, and grated ginger to ground pork and stir-fry until flaky) ······ as needed

Cheese slice ······ 1 slice

Deep-fried pasta ······ as needed

Kamaboko fish cake ······ small amount

Nori sheet ······ as needed

Dark-pink soft salami ······ 1 slice

 He's sticking his tongue out at you!

Pluto

BENTO MENU

Bell pepper meat roll ▸p.88

Simmered pumpkin ▸p.91

Dog's footprint mark (punch holes on a sausage with a straw and fill in cheese slice ③ to create a foot pattern; see Mickey Logo Sausage on p. 75)

Edamame pick, carrot star, broccoli, lettuce, rice

INGREDIENTS

Ingredient	Amount
Rice	0.9 oz./25 g
Pumpkin (cooked in microwave)	as needed
Nori sheet	small amount
Cheese slice	½ slice
Thinly sliced carrots (boiled in salted water)	small amount
Snow peas in the pod (boiled in salted water)	small amount

RECIPE

Paper Pattern Template p. 43

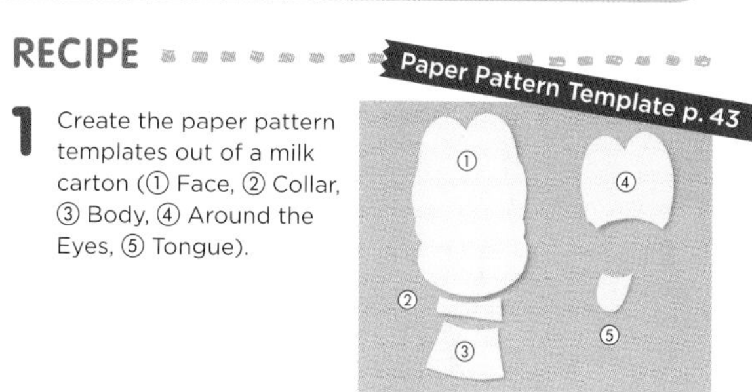

1 Create the paper pattern templates out of a milk carton (① Face, ② Collar, ③ Body, ④ Around the Eyes, ⑤ Tongue).

2 Pack around half of the bento box with rice at an angle and fill in the open area with the side dishes and vegetables.

3 Mix 0.9 oz./25 g of rice with mashed pumpkin and add a little salt to taste.

4 Separate the seasoned rice from **3** into two portions: 0.7 oz./20 g for the face and the remaining 0.18 oz./5 g for the body. Mold them into the shape of paper templates ① and ③. Place them onto the packed rice from **2**.

5 Trace the shapes of the nose, right ear, and left ear on baking paper, place it on top of two overlapping nori sheets, and cut them out to create two of each piece.

6 Use a toothpick to cut around the contour of the nose on a cheese slice. Glue the nose nori sheet from step **5** to both sides of the cheese slice. Also, create the right and left ears using the same method and glue the ears onto **4**.

ATTENTION! If you glue the nori onto only the top side of the cheese nose, the cheese will start to curl up, so glue nori onto the back side of the cheese as well to prevent curling.

7 Place paper template ④ on the cheese slice, cut around its contour, and place the cheese onto the face.

8 Trace the eyes, mouth, and lines of the chin onto baking paper, place it over a nori sheet, cut the shapes out, and glue them onto the face.

9 Place paper template ⑤ on the carrot, cut around it, and place the tongue on the face. Cut a thin strip of nori sheet for the line in the center of the tongue and glue it onto the tongue.

10 Place paper template ③ on the snow pea and cut around it. Place the collar onto the body.

MICKEY MOUSE & FRIENDS **The beret and the lifebuoy ring add a maritime look!**

Donald Duck

BENTO MENU

Deep-fried chicken tenders with almonds ▸p. 88

Japanese omelette ▸p. 91

Floating tube fish cake, carrot stars, broccoli, snow peas, cherry tomato, lettuce, corn pilaf (you should be able to find floating tube fish cake in any Asian market)

INGREDIENTS

- **Ham** .... 1 slice
- **Cheese slice** .... 1 slice
- **Thin omelette sheet** .... small amount
- **Nori sheet** .... as needed
- **Green pepper** (cooked in microwave) .... ¼
- **Thinly sliced carrot** (boiled in salted water) .... small amount

RECIPE

1

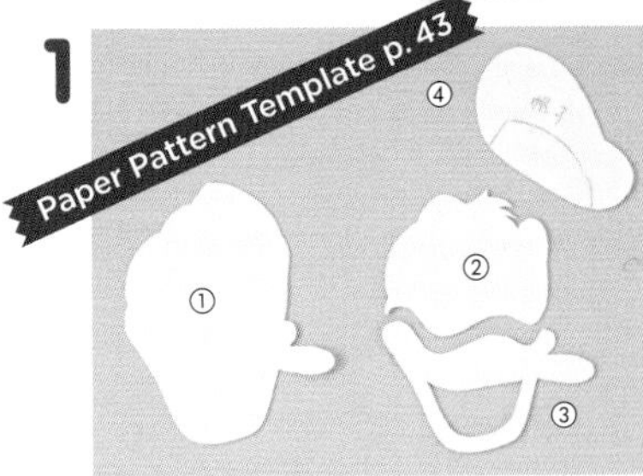

Create the paper pattern templates out of a milk carton (① Outline of the Face, ② Upper Face, ③ Beak, ④ Hat).

2 Place paper template ① on the ham and cut around it.

3 Place paper template ② on the cheese slice, use a toothpick to cut around it, and place it onto **2**.

4 Place paper template ③ on the thin omelette sheet, cut around it, and place it on the bottom of **3**.

5 Trace the eyebrows, the line around the eyes, the pupils, the outline of the right side of the face, the lines of the beak, and the lines for the hat onto baking paper, place it on top of the nori sheet to cut the shapes out, and glue them onto the face. The lines for the hat are glued onto the top of the ham from **2**.

6 Place paper template ④ on the green pepper and cut around it. Place the hat onto the corn pilaf that has been packed into the bento box and then place **5** onto the pilaf as well.

ATTENTION! Donald's hat is green in this bento, so using a blue bento box and blue toothpick will really make your marine theme pop!

7 Trace the ribbon for the hat onto baking paper, place it on top of two overlapping nori sheets, and cut it out to create two of them.

8 Glue one of the ribbons from **7** onto the cheese slice, cut around it using a toothpick, and glue the other nori ribbon on its back. Place the ribbon on the left edge of the hat from **6**.

9 Cut the carrot into a triangular shape for the tongue and place it onto the mouth.

BENTO MENU

Sweet potato and raisin salad ▸p.92

Purple sweet potato flowers (omelette sheet in the middle), **fruits** (grape, orange, pink grapefruit, kiwi), **broccoli, cherry tomato, lettuce**

INGREDIENTS

Sandwich bread	2 slices
Favorite sandwich filling	as needed
Thin omelette sheet	small amount
Loin ham	1 slice
Cheese slice	½ slice
Nori sheet	as needed
Thinly sliced carrot (boiled in salted water)	small amount

MICKEY MOUSE & FRIENDS **She's adorable!**

Daisy Duck

RECIPE

1 Paper Pattern Template p. 43

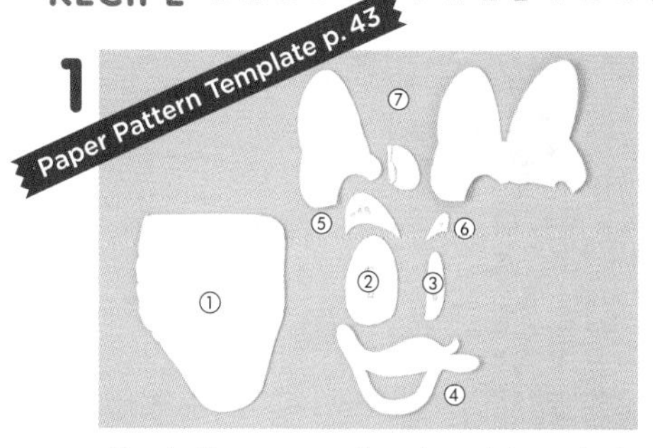

Create the paper pattern templates out of a milk carton (① Outline of the Face, ② Right Eye, ③ Left Eye, ④ Beak, ⑤ Right Eyelid, ⑥ Left Eyelid, ⑦ Ribbon).

2 Place paper template ① on the sandwich bread, cut out two slices, and add your favorite fillings to create a sandwich. Place them into the bento box with other side dishes and vegetables.

ATTENTION! It will be easier to use a knife to cut out a rough shape of the face first and then trim it with scissors.

3 Place paper template ④ on the thin omelette sheet and cut around it.

4 Place **3** on top of the ham and cut along the outline. Be careful to not cut through the inside of the mouth or hollow out the tongue area. Attach the ham and omelette sheet onto the face.

5 Place paper templates ② and ③ on the cheese slice, cut around them with a toothpick, and place them onto the face.

6 Place paper templates ⑤, ⑥, and, ⑦ on the loin ham, cut around them, and place them on the face.

7 Trace the eyes, eyelashes, eyebrows and lines of the beak onto baking paper, place it over a nori sheet, cut the shapes out, and glue them onto the face.

8 Cut the carrot into a triangular shape for the tongue and place it onto the mouth.

MICKEY MOUSE & FRIENDS

Mickey & Minnie

The perfect couple! All smiles here!

BENTO MENU

Mayo-teriyaki chicken ▸p.88

Simmered tri-color veggies ▸p.93

Heart-shaped sausage (cut a red sausage diagonally in half, flip one side over, and attach the cut ends together with deep-fried pasta)

Ketchup rice ball,* boiled asparagus, lettuce

*To make the ketchup rice ball, mix around 1 oz./30 of cooked rice with 1 tablespoon of ketchup and a little soy sauce. You can add more ketchup to adjust the color of the rice. Separate the rice into two portions and use cling wrap to shape them into ovals.

INGREDIENTS

Nori sheet .... as needed
Cheese slice .... 1 slice
Thinly sliced kamaboko fish cake .... small amount
Ham .... ¼ slice

RECIPE

Paper Pattern Template p. 43

1 Copy Mickey onto the baking paper.

2 Place **1** on top of two sheets of nori and cut around the contour.

3 Glue one of the nori from **2** onto the cheese slice. Use a toothpick to cut around it and glue the other nori Mickey on the back.

ATTENTION! Gluing nori on both sides will prevent the cheese from curling.

4 Trace Mickey's face onto a sheet of baking paper and cut it out as a template. Place the template on top of the cheese and trace the contour with a toothpick.

5 Place **4** on top of **3**.

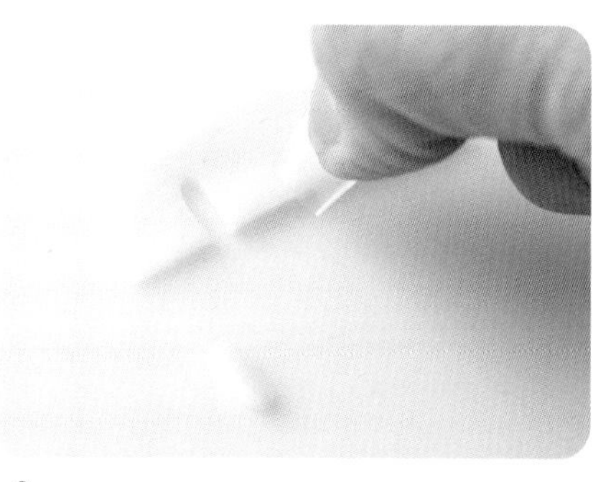

6 Squeeze a straw to punch the eyes out of the fish cake and place them onto **5**.

7 Place the baking paper template from **4** on a nori sheet to cut out the eyes, the line under the eyes, the nose, and the mouth. Glue them onto **6**.

8 Repeat steps **1–7** to make Minnie.

9 Cut thin strips of nori for the eyelashes and glue them onto **8**.

10 Cut the ribbon out of the baking paper with Minnie, place it on top of the ham, and cut around it.

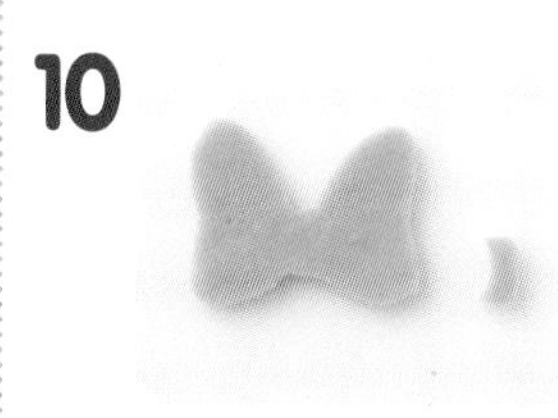

11 Place the ribbon from **10** onto Minnie.

MICKEY MOUSE & FRIENDS

Goofy

The hair poking out of his hat makes an impression! There's a hidden Mickey too!

BENTO MENU

Sausage star, fruits (grape, blueberries, pineapple, kiwi, pink grapefruit), **broccoli, lettuce, ham and egg salad sandwich**

INGREDIENTS

- **Cheddar cheese** ..... ½ slice
- **Ham** ..... 1 slice
- **Snap peas** (boiled in salted water) ..... 1 pod
- **Nori sheet** ..... as needed
- **Cheese slice** ..... small amount

RECIPE

1

Paper Pattern Template p. 44

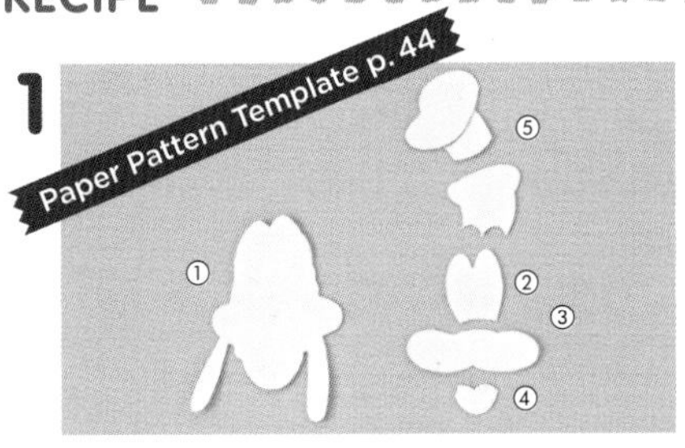

Create the paper pattern templates out of a milk carton (① Outline of the Face, ② Around the Eyes, ③ Around the Nose, ④ Tongue, ⑤ Hat Pieces).

2 Place paper template ① on the cheddar cheese, cut around it with a toothpick, and place the cheese on top of a piece of loin ham.

3 Place paper template ⑤ on the snap pea and cut around it to make Goofy's hat. Place the hat on top of the ham from **2**. Trim the ham by cutting around the contour of the face while leaving the ham edges showing.

4 Trace the face (the dark area of Goofy's head), right ear, left ear, and mouth onto the baking paper, place it over a nori sheet to cut the shapes out, and glue them onto the cheddar cheese from **2**.

5 Place paper template ③ on the cheddar cheese, use a toothpick to cut around it, and place it onto the face.

6 Slightly squeeze a straw to punch out an oval shape from the cheese, and then use the straw to cut the oval in half to form the shape of Goofy's teeth.

7 Place paper template ④ on the ham, cut around it, and place the tongue onto the mouth.

8 Trace the eyes, nose, tongue, hair, and line for the hat onto the baking paper, place it over a nori sheet to cut the shapes out, and glue them onto the face.

9 Pack the bento box with the sandwich, side dishes, and vegetables, and place **8** on top of it.

BENTO MENU

- Japanese omelette ▶p.91
- Carrots râpées ▶p.93
- **Sausage acorns** (attach half a meatball and the tip of a sausage or frankfurter together with deep-fried pasta)
- **Radish mushroom** (recipe below)
- **Cherry tomato, broccoli, snap peas in the pod, lettuce**

INGREDIENTS

Rice ··· 3.5 oz./100 g

CHIP

Bonito rice seasoning* ··· as needed

DALE

Japanese noodle soup base* ··· as needed

Cheese slice ··· 1 slice

Kamaboko fish cake ··· small amount

Little smokie ··· ½ sausage

Nori sheet ··· as needed

Sausage or frankfurter ··· ½ sausage

Pasta ··· as needed

*You can find both the bonito rice seasoning and the Japanese noodle soup base in Japanese and other Asian supermarkets. The bonito seasoning is usually labeled as "furikake," and the Japanese noodle soup base is labeled as "metsuyu." If you can't find either of these products in your nearby grocery store, you can dilute soy sauce with water or mirin to create the desired color.

CHIP & DALE **The perfect duo!**

Chip & Dale

RECIPE

1

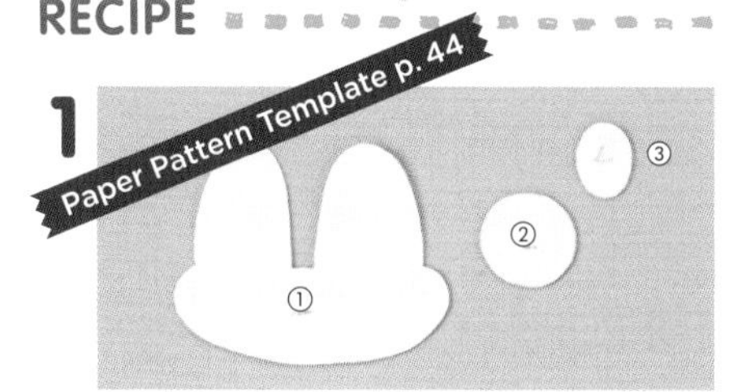

Create the paper pattern templates out of a milk carton (① Chip's Face, ② Around the Mouth, ③ Eye).

2 Split the rice into two portions of 1.8 oz./50 g. Sprinkle one portion with bonito seasoning and mix the other rice with the noodle soup base. (The bonito rice ball will be Chip and the soup base rice ball will be Dale.) Mold them into a circular shape and pack them into the bento box with the other side dishes and vegetables.

ATTENTION! They'll look even cuter if you place the two faces close to each other.

3 Place paper template ① on the cheese slice and use a toothpick to cut two of them out. Place one on top of the bonito seasoning rice ball and flip the other cheese face over and place it on the noodle soup base rice ball.

4 Place paper template ② on the fish cake, cut two of them out, and place them onto each of the faces.

5 Place paper template ③ on the fish cake, cut four of them out, and place them on the faces..

6 Cut off the tip of a little smokie as the nose and place it on Dale's face.

7 Trace Chip's eyebrows, eyes, nose, and mouth, and Dale's forelock, eyes, mouth, and teeth onto the baking paper, place it over a nori sheet to cut the shapes out, and glue them onto each of the faces.

8 Cut 0.4 inch/1 cm off from the end of a sausage or frankfurter and slice it into four pieces for the ears. Then attach them to the head with the pasta.

9 Cut thin strips off from the remaining sausage or frankfurter as eyebrows for Dale and place them above the eyes.

RADISH MUSHROOM

1. Cut off the leaves and root of the radish. From the leaf side of the radish, shove the thin end of the round piping tip into the radish until it reaches the center
2. Use a knife to cut around the piping tip in 1. Remove the radish around the piping tip to create the stem.
3. Use a smaller piping tip to create circular marks on the surface of the radish. Peel off the radish skin in the circular areas.

BENTO MENU

Flower pattern meat roll ▸p.88

Sautéed potato and corn ▸p.93

Honey pot sausage (recipe below), fish sausage with bee on a pick (recipe below), carrot butterflies, broccoli, asparagus, cherry tomato, lettuce

INGREDIENTS

Fish sausage (0.2 inch/5 mm slice)	2 slices
Ketchup chicken rice	3.5 oz./100 g
Cheese slice	1 slice
Thin omelette sheet	1 sheet
Nori sheet	as needed
Pasta	as needed

WINNIE THE POOH

Pooh's gentle expression is so relaxing!
The cute side dishes make it look like he's in a field of flowers!

Winnie the Pooh

RECIPE

Paper Pattern Template p. 44

1

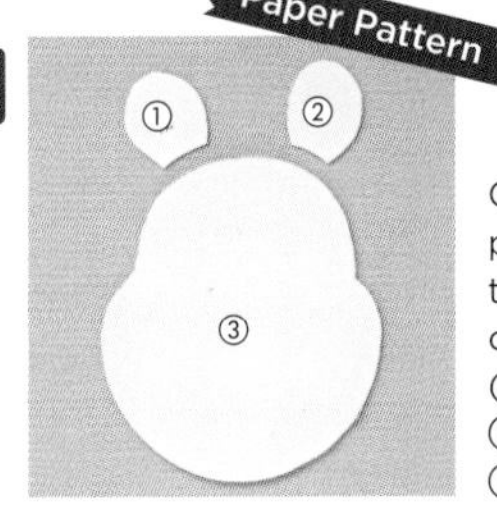

Create the paper pattern templates out of a milk carton (① Right Ear, ② Left Ear, ③ Face).

2 Place paper templates ① and ② on the fish sausage to cut out the shapes. Use the same templates to cut out the shapes from the omelette sheet and place them on top of the fish sausage.

3 Gently mold the ketchup chicken rice to the shape of the face on paper template ③.

4 Place paper template ③ on the cheese slice and cut it with a toothpick. Place the cheese slice on top of the ketchup chicken rice from **3** and cover it with the thin omelette sheet. Place cling wrap on top to shape the face.

ATTENTION! The cheese slice keeps the egg color looking yellow and prevents the red color of the fried rice from showing.

5 Place **4**, the other side dishes, and the vegetables into the bento box.

6 Trace the eyebrows, eyes, ridges of the nose, mouth, and chin on the baking paper, place it over a nori sheet, and cut out the shapes. Glue them onto the face.

7 Attach the ears from **2** onto the head using pasta.

HONEY POT SAUSAGE

Cut a 2 cm/1 inch piece of little smokie from the edge as the honey pot. From the other side of the little smokie, cut off a thin slice (1 mm/ 0.1 inch), and then cut a 0.12 inch/3 mm slice as the lid. Use a toothpick to cut cheddar cheese in the shape of the dripping honey and place it onto the honey pot. Use a cocktail pick to attach the lid to the pot.

FISH SAUSAGE WITH BEE ON A PICK

Cut two slices off from the fish sausage and thread them with a toothpick. Place the bee (p. 80) and flower (the petals are made of a slice of white cheese like Monterey Jack or white cheddar and the center is cheddar cheese) on the sausage slices.

WINNIE THE POOH **Just lying around and relaxing!**

Piglet

BENTO MENU

- Carrot and pork patty ▸p.89
- Asparagus sautéed with herbs ▸p.91
- Sunflower sausage (recipe below)
- Carrot flower, cherry tomato, lettuce, rice

INGREDIENTS

Ham	1 slice
Dark-pink soft salami	½ slice
Nori sheet	as needed

RECIPE

1 Paper Pattern Template p. 44

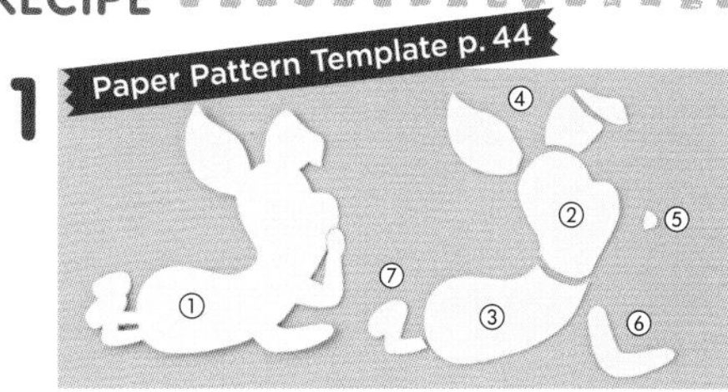

Create the paper pattern templates out of a milk carton (① Outline, ② Face, ③ Body, ④ Ears, ⑤ Nose, ⑥ Right Hand, ⑦ Right Leg).

2 Place paper templates ①, ②, ⑥, and ⑦ on the ham and cut around it.

3 Place paper templates ③, ④, and ⑤ on the soft salami and cut around it. After cutting the body shape out of the soft salami, use the curve of the heart-shaped cutter to cut the body into several pieces so the ham underneath is slightly visible and looks like stripes. If you don't have a cutter, use a knife.

4 Place the face, body, ears, nose, right hand, and right leg onto the ham outline from **2** in that order.

5 Trace the eyebrows, ridges of the nose, and mouth onto the baking paper, place it over a nori sheet to cut the shapes out, and glue them onto the face.

6 Pack half of the bento box with rice at an angle, fill the open area with the side dishes and vegetables, and place **5** on the rice.

SUNFLOWER SAUSAGE

1. Fold half of a thin omelette sheet lengthwise. Make small inserts on the folded edge about 0.2 inch/5 mm apart from each other.
2. Score the frankfurter and wrap it with the egg from 1. Fix the egg to the frankfurter with a piece of fried pasta.

WINNIE THE POOH

Pooh & Tigger

These will keep you in good cheer!

BENTO MENU

- Colorful patty ▸p.89
- Simmered tri-color veggies ▸p.93
- Bee ▸p.80
- Thin omelette sheet dandelion, lettuce, boiled asparagus, snap peas

INGREDIENTS

POOH

Rice	1.8 oz./50 g
Pumpkin (cooked in microwave)	as needed
Deep-fried pasta	as needed
Nori sheet	as needed

TIGGER

Rice	1.8 oz./50 g
Ketchup	as needed
Deep-fried pasta	as needed
Cheese slice	as needed
Ham	small amount
Nori sheet	as needed

RECIPE

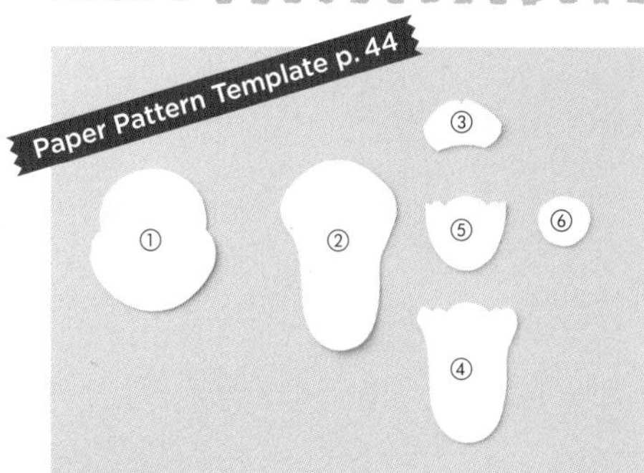

1 Create the paper pattern templates out of a milk carton (① Pooh's Face, ② Tigger's Face, ③ Around Tigger's Eyes, ④ Around Tigger's Mouth, ⑤ Around Tigger's Nose, ⑥ Tigger's Nose).

2 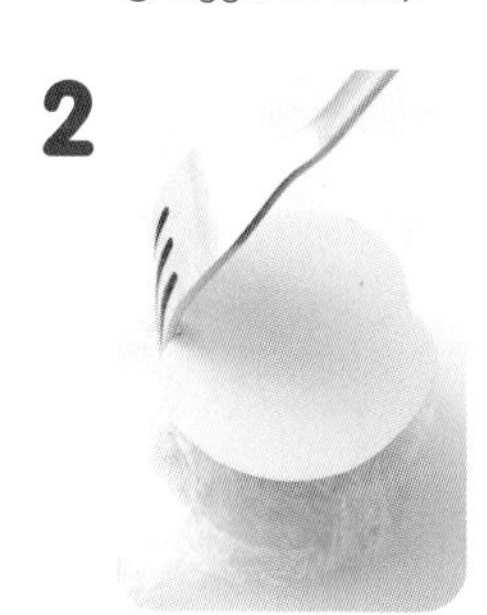

Mix 1.8 oz./50 g of the rice with mashed pumpkin and add a little salt to taste. Leave a small amount (0.1 oz./3 g) of rice and mold the rest into the shape of Pooh's face on paper template ①.

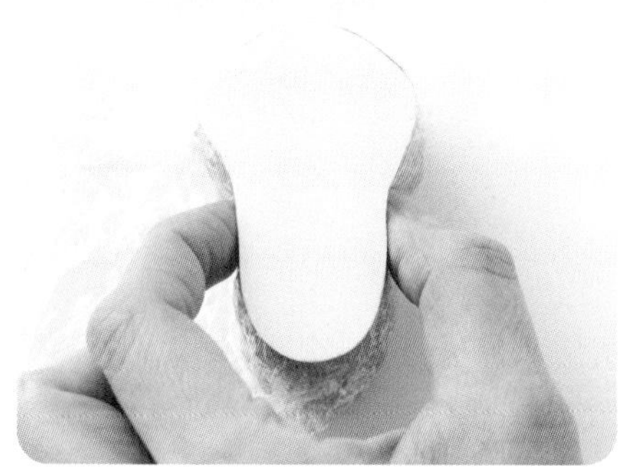

3 Mix ketchup and a pinch of salt into 1.8 oz./50 g of rice. Microwave rice uncovered for about 20 seconds to get rid of the moisture. Mix well again, leave a small amount (0.14 oz./4 g) of rice, and gently mold the rest into the shape of Tigger's face. Adjust the shape of the face using paper template ②.

4 Place **2** and **3** into the bento box with the other side dishes and vegetables.

ATTENTION! Place the faces close to each other to make them look even friendlier.

5 Divide the remaining rice from **2** and **3** in half and mold these portions into the shape of Pooh's and Tigger's ears.

6 Attach the ears onto the face rice ball with deep-fried pasta.

7 Use a toothpick to cut around paper templates ③, ④, and ⑤ on the cheese slice. Place them onto the face.

8 Place paper template ⑥ on the ham, cut around it, and place the nose onto the cheese slice face.

9 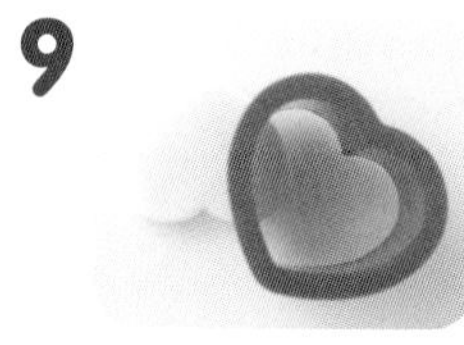

Use a heart-shaped cutter to punch a heart out of the cheese slice. Move the heart-shaped cutter a bit, punch down upon the heart to cut out the shapes of the inside of Tigger's ears, and place them on the ears.

Note: If you don't have a heart shaped cutter, trace the shape of the inside of Tigger's ears onto baking paper and use toothpicks to cut the cheese slice into the ear shape.

10 Trace Pooh's face (eyebrows, eyes, lines above the nose, nose, mouth, chin line) and Tigger's face (patterns onto the face, eyebrows, eyes, lines around the nose, patterns on the cheeks) onto a piece of baking paper. Place the paper over a nori sheet, cut the shapes out, and glue them onto the faces.

FROZEN

Elsa & Anna

The dignified expression on their faces gives you courage!

Elsa

BENTO MENU

Mayo-teriyaki chicken ▸p.88

Sweet potato simmered in lemon juice ▸p.92

Pasta flower, cherry tomato, broccoli, okra, lettuce, rice

INGREDIENTS

Chicken or turkey breast	1 slice
Thin omelette sheet (less yolk)	½ sheet
Snow pea (boiled in salted water)	1 pod
Cheese slice	small amount
Kelp	small amount
Little smokie casing	small amount
Nori sheet	as needed

1

Paper Pattern Template p. 45

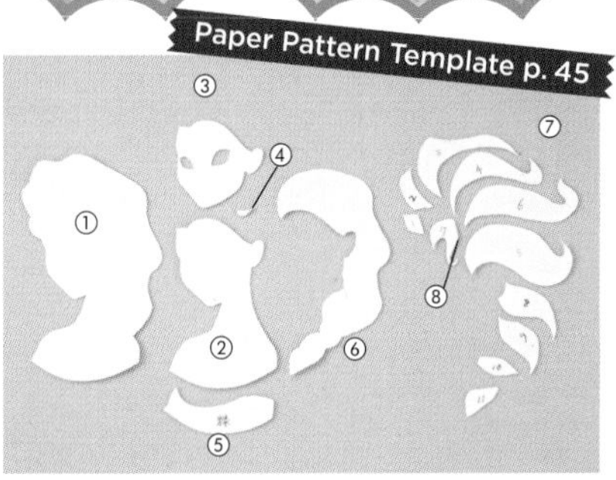

Create the paper pattern templates out of a milk carton (① Outline, ② Face/Body, ③ Face with Eyes Cut Out, ④ Mouth, ⑤ Clothes, ⑥ Hair, ⑦ Pieces of the Hair, ⑧ Front Hair).

2

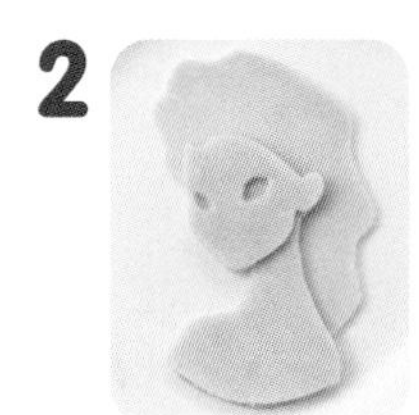

Place paper templates ①, ②, and ③ on the chicken or turkey breast and cut around the template. Place the face/body piece on top of the outline ham and then place it on the face.

ATTENTION! The outline piece can secure other face and hair pieces and prevent them from sliding. It also makes the character more vivid.

3 Cut the thin omelette sheet (less yolk) along paper templates ⑥ and ⑦ and place them on the outline from **2**. Cut the snow pea along paper template ⑤ and place it on the body.

4 Place paper template ③ on top of the cheese slice and cut around the inside of the eyes. Place the cheese pieces in the holes of the eyes of the chicken or turkey ham. Cut thin strips of kelp for the eyebrows and place them on the face.

5 Cut the casing of a little smokie along paper template ④ and place it on the face. Cut the thin omelette sheet (less yolk) using paper template ⑧ and place it on top of the hair.

6

Cut a thin strip off of nori for the nose, glue it onto the face, and adjust its placement with a toothpick.

7 Use a round piping tip to punch out two round shapes from the snow pea. Move the piping tip a little to punch out the eyes from the round shapes and place them onto the eyes. Trace the eyelashes and pupil onto baking paper, place it over a nori sheet to cut them out, and glue them onto the eyes.

8 Use a round piping tip to punch out the light in the eyes and place them onto the eyes.

9 Pack around half of the bento box with rice. Fill the other half with the side dishes and vegetables, and place **8** onto the rice.

Anna

BENTO MENU

Cod wrapped in bacon ▸p.90

Pumpkin and sweet potato salad ▸p.91

Pasta flower, broccoli, cherry tomato, lettuce, rice

INGREDIENTS

Chicken or turkey breast	1 slice
Thin omelette sheet with brown sugar	½ sheet
Dark-pink soft salami	1 slice
Cheese slice	small amount
Kelp	small amount
Little smokie casing	small amount
Nori sheet	as needed
Snow pea (boiled in salted water)	small amount

1

Paper Pattern Template p. 45

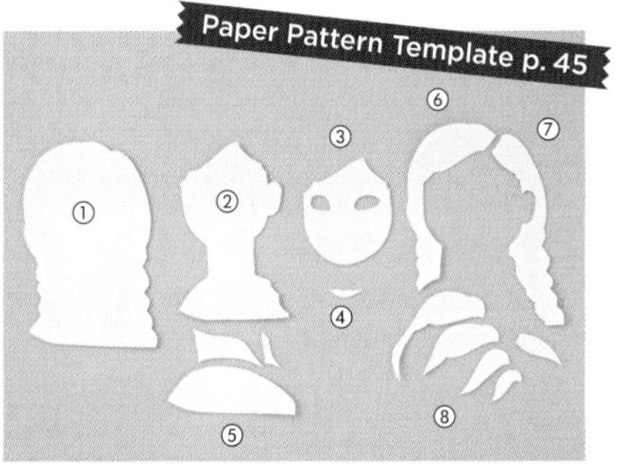

Create the paper pattern templates out of a milk carton (① Outline, ② Face/Body, ③ Face with Eyes Cut Out, ④ Mouth, ⑤ Parts of the Clothes, ⑥ Right Hair, ⑦ Left Hair, ⑧ Front Hair Parts).

2 Place paper templates ①, ②, and ③ on a piece of chicken or turkey breast and cut around the template. Place the face/body piece on the outline ham and then put it on the face piece.

3

Cut the omelette sheet (less yolk) along paper templates ⑥ and ⑦ and place them on the outline from **2** .

4 Place paper template ⑤ onto the soft salami, cut around it, and glue the pieces onto the body. Place paper template ③ on top of the cheese slice and cut around the inside of the eyes with a toothpick. Place the cheese pieces in the holes of the eyes of the chicken or turkey breast.

5 Cut thin strips of kelp for the eyebrows and place them on the face. Cut the casing of a little smokie along paper template ④ and place it on the face.

6 Cut a thin strip off the nori sheet for the nose, glue it to the face, and adjust its place with a toothpick. Cut the brown sugar omelette sheet using paper template ⑧ and place the pieces onto the head.

7 Use a round piping tip to punch out two round shapes from the snow pea. Move the piping tip a little to punch out the eyes from the round shapes and place them on the eyes. Trace the eyelashes and pupil onto baking paper, place the paper over a nori sheet to cut the eye pieces out, and glue them onto the eyes. Cut thin strips off the nori sheet and glue them onto the hair to create a braid-like pattern.

8 Use a round piping tip to punch out the light in the eyes and place them on the eyes. Cut out a lock of white hair from the remaining cheese slice and place it on the braid on the right.

9 Pack around half of the bento box with rice, fill the other half with the side dishes, and place ⑧ onto the rice.

FROZEN

The happy snowman!

Olaf

BENTO MENU

- Sautéed sausage and mushrooms ▶p.89
- Mayonnaise prawn ▶p.90
- Pumpkin and sweet potato salad ▶p.91
- Pasta flower, broccoli, lettuce

INGREDIENTS

Rice	3.5 oz./100 g
Cheese slice	small amount
Nori sheet	as needed
Thinly sliced carrots (boiled in salted water)	small amount
Snack kelp*	small amount

*You can find snack kelp in Japanese supermarkets. Alternatively, you can use kelp jerky or meat jerky with a soft texture.

RECIPE

1 Paper Pattern Template p. 45

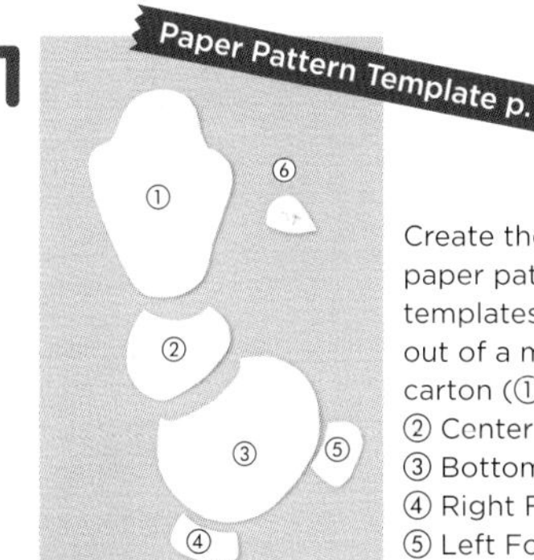

Create the paper pattern templates out of a milk carton (① Face, ② Center Body, ③ Bottom Body, ④ Right Foot, ⑤ Left Foot, ⑥ Nose).

2 Separate the rice into a 1.4 oz./40 g portion (face), a 0.35 oz./10 g portion (center body), and a 1.23 oz./35 g portion (bottom body). Split the remaining 0.53 oz./15 g into two portions for the feet.

Mold the rice portions into the shape of paper templates ①, ②, ③, ④, and ⑤, and pack them into the bento box along with the other side dishes and vegetables.

ATTENTION! Placing the feet on top of the side dishes will prevent them from falling down to the bottom of the box.

3 Use a round cutter to punch the eyes out of the cheese slice and place them on the face. If you don't have a round cutter, trace the shape of the eye on a milk carton and use a toothpick to cut off the cheese in the same shape.

4 Trace the eyebrows, eyes, mouth, and body patterns onto baking paper, place it over a nori sheet to cut the shapes out, and glue them onto the character.

5 Place paper template ⑥ on the carrot, cut around it, and place it on the face.

6 Cut the cheese slice into a rectangle for the tooth and place it on the mouth.

7

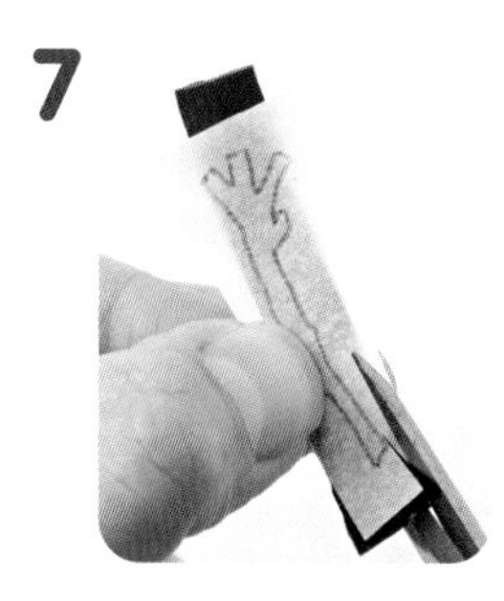

Trace the hands onto baking paper, place it over a snack kelp, and cut it into the shapes of the hands. Cut out thin strips from the remaining snack kelp and stick them into the rice ball as hair.

OSWALD THE LUCKY RABBIT **His smile is contagious!**

Oswald

BENTO MENU

Broccoli, cherry tomato, hot dog, potato salad sandwich

INGREDIENTS

Nori sheet	as needed
Cheese slice	1 slice
Ham	1 slice

RECIPE

Paper Pattern Template p. 45

1. Trace the illustration on a piece of baking paper, place it over the nori sheet, and cut along the illustration with a garnishing knife.

   ATTENTION! If the nori tears while you are cutting it, don't worry—you can stick it back together when you glue it onto the cheese.

2. Glue **1** onto the cheese slice and use a toothpick to trim the cheese slice to make it slightly bigger than the nori parts.

3. Place **2** on top of the ham and cut around the cheese.

   ATTENTION! By placing a layer of ham under the cheese, you can prevent the cheese from curling and getting soggy.

4. Pack the bento box with the hot dog, potato salad sandwich, and vegetables, and place **3** on top of it.

101 DALMATIANS **The droopy ears are so cute!**

Lucky

BENTO MENU

Colorful patty ▸p.89

Simmered chikuwa fish cake and vegetables ▸p.91

Footprints (place the cheddar cheese on top of the ham slice, punch through it with a round piping tip, and glue pieces of nori that have been cut out in the shape of a footprint)

Thin omelette sheet dandelion, snap pea pods, lettuce, broccoli

INGREDIENTS

Rice	3.5 oz./100 g
Nori sheet	as needed
Cheese slice	½ slice
Ham	small amount

RECIPE

1 Paper Pattern Template p. 45

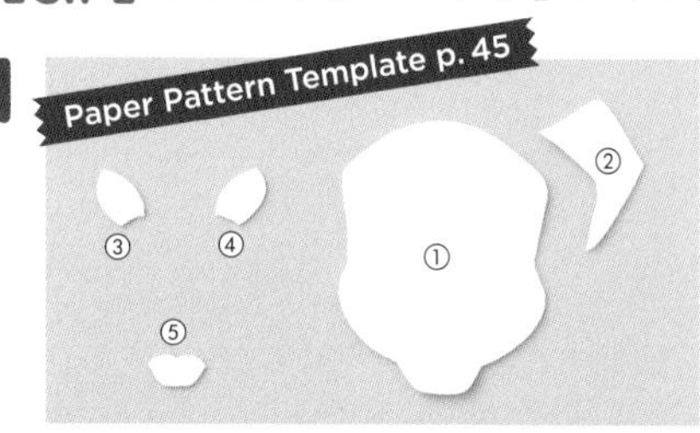

Create the paper pattern templates out of a milk carton (① Face, ② Back of Left Ear, ③ Right Eye, ④ Left Eye, ⑤ Tongue).

2 Separate the rice into two portions: the face (3.2 oz./90 g) and the back of the left ear (0.35 oz./10 g). Mold them into the shape of paper templates ① and ②.

3 

Cut a rectangular piece of nori as the back side of the left ear and glue it onto the left ear rice ball. Pack the rice balls into the bento box along with the other side dishes and vegetables.

ATTENTION! The ear will look more three-dimensional if you make the back of the ear and the drooping part separately.

4 Trace the nose onto baking paper, place it over two overlapping nori sheets, and cut out the nose.

5 Glue one of the nori slices from **4** onto the cheese slice, cut around it with a toothpick, and glue the remaining nori slice onto the back of the cheese. Place the nose on the face.

6 Trace the right ear and the drooping part of the left ear on baking paper, create the ears in the same process as **4** and **5**, and place them where the ears should be.

7 Place paper templates ③ and ④ on the cheese slice, cut around them with a toothpick, and place them on the face.

8 Trace the eyebrows, mouth, and spots on the head on a piece of baking paper. Place it over a nori sheet to cut the shapes out, and then glue them onto the face.

9 Cut thin strips of nori to create the lines of the nose and eyes and glue them onto the face.

10 Place paper template ⑤ on the ham, cut around it, and place the tongue on the mouth.

BENTO MENU

Mayo-teriyaki chicken ▸p.88

Sautéed sausage with bell peppers ▸p.89

Mashed sweet potato pineapple
(wrap bite-size cheese* with the mashed sweet potato, create lines with a knife, and attach a cut snow pea on top)

Cherry tomato, broccoli, snap pea pod, lettuce

*The bite-size cheese can be found in Japanese supermarkets. It's labeled as "candy cheese." You can also substitute a small mozzarella cheese ball (bocconcini).

INGREDIENTS

Dinner roll	1 roll
Favorite sandwich filling	as needed
Cheese slice	½ slice
Nori sheet	as needed
Ham	1 slice
Sausage or frankfurter	1 slice

LILO & STITCH **It looks like Stitch is going to jump out of the bento!**

Stitch

RECIPE

1 
Paper Pattern Template p. 46

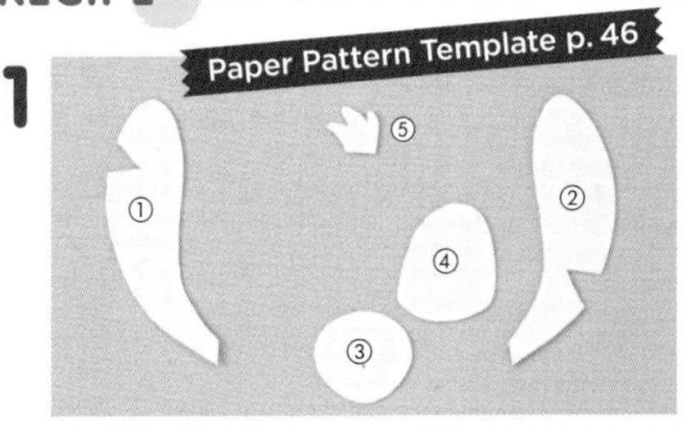

Create the paper pattern templates out of a milk carton (① Right Ear, ② Left Ear, ③ Nose, ④ Eyes, ⑤ Hair).

2 Create a slit on the side of the dinner roll and fill it with your favorite fillings.

3 Make a shallow cut on the surface of the roll (about 0.4 inch/1 cm from the edge). Peel off the outer skin (the light-brown part) to create the mouth and pack it into the bento box with the other side dishes and vegetables.

4 Place paper template ③ on the cheese slice. Cut around it and place the nose onto the dinner roll.

5 Place paper template ④ on the cheese slice, cut two eyes out, and place them on the face (flip one over to use as the opposite eye).

6 Trace the nose, pupils, and lines on the top of the eyes on a piece of baking paper, place it over a nori sheet to cut the shapes out, and glue them onto the face.

7 Punch out the lights in the eyes from the cheese slice with a slightly squeezed straw and place them on the pupils.

8 Place paper templates ① and ② on the ham and cut around it. Place the bottom of the ear in between the bread and the side dishes and vegetables.

9 Place paper template ⑤ on the sliced skinless sausage and cut around it. Create a slit on top of the dinner roll and put the sausage hair piece in place.

FINDING NEMO **Cute eyes!**

Nemo

BENTO MENU

Sautéed spinach with sakura shrimp ▸p.93

Lotus root dressed with cod roe ▸p.94

Lunch meat shell, thin omelette sheet dandelion, bell pepper fish, Italian parsley seaweed, broccoli, lettuce, seaweed rice*

*To make seaweed rice, simply mix the rice with a little seaweed furikake. Seaweed furikake can be found in Asian supermarkets and some local grocery stores. If you can't find the seaweed furikake, you can break seaweed snacks into pieces and mix it with the rice.

INGREDIENTS

Ham ········ 1 slice
Thin omelette sheet with ketchup ········ ½ slice
Nori sheet ········ as needed
Cheese slice ········ small amount

RECIPE

Paper Pattern Template p. 46

1 Create the paper pattern templates out of a milk carton (① Outline, ② Body with Abdominal Fin and Tail Fin, ③ Pectoral Fin, ④ Back Fin, ⑤ Back Fin Pattern, ⑥ Body Pattern).

2 Place paper template ① on the ham and cut around it.

3 
Place paper templates ②, Body, ③, and ④ on the ketchup omelette sheet and cut around them.

4 Place **3** on **2**.

5 
Trace the patterns on the body (the black part) on a piece of baking paper. Place it over a nori sheet to cut out the shapes and glue them onto the body from **2**.

6 Place paper templates ⑤ and ⑥ on the cheese slice and cut around them with a toothpick. Use a round piping tip to punch out the eyes and place everything onto the body from **2**.

7 Trace the eyebrows, pupils, and mouth on a piece of baking paper. Place it over a nori sheet to cut the shapes out and glue them onto the body from **2**.

8 Cut thin strips of nori for the lines on the fins and glue them onto the fins.

9 Use a round piping tip to punch out the lights in the eyes from the cheese slice and place them on the pupils.

10 Pack half of the bento box with seaweed rice. Fill the open area with the side dishes and vegetables and place **9** on top of the rice.

BIG HERO 6 **Baymax is always there for his friends!**

Baymax

BENTO MENU

Prawn and broccoli mayo salad ▸p. 90

Fruits (mandarin orange, grape), okra, lettuce

INGREDIENTS

Sandwich bread	2 slices
Favorite sandwich filling	as needed
Nori sheet	as needed

RECIPE

1 Paper Pattern Template p. 46

Create the paper pattern template out of a milk carton (① Face).

2 Lightly moisten the bread with a spray of water and heat in the microwave for about ten seconds.

3

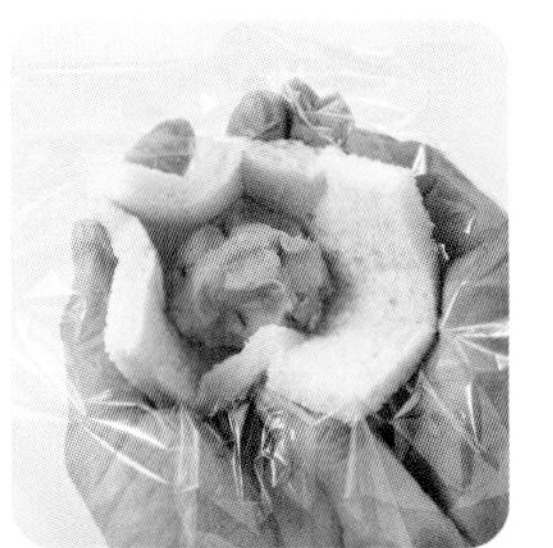

Create two 0.8 inch/2 cm cuts on all four sides of the bread and place it on top of a piece of cling wrap. Put your favorite filling on top of the bread and wrap it into a round shape. Mold the sandwich to the shape of paper template ①.

4 Place the sandwich into the bento box along with the other side dishes and vegetables.

5 Trace Baymax's eyes and the soccer ball pattern onto a piece of baking paper, place it over a nori sheet, and cut the shapes out.

6 Spread a small amount of honey on the back of the nori pieces from **5** and glue them onto the sandwiches.

PLANES **Soar through the sky!**

Dusty

BENTO MENU

- Colorful patty ▸p.89
- Simmered chikuwa fish cake and vegetables ▸p.91
- Thin omelette sheet dandelion, cheese clouds, broccoli, lettuce, rice

INGREDIENTS

- Ham ········ 1 slice
- Cheese slice ········ 1 slice
- Thin omelette sheet with ketchup ········ ½ slice
- Nori sheet ········ as needed
- Broccoli stem (boiled in salted water) ··· small amount

RECIPE

1

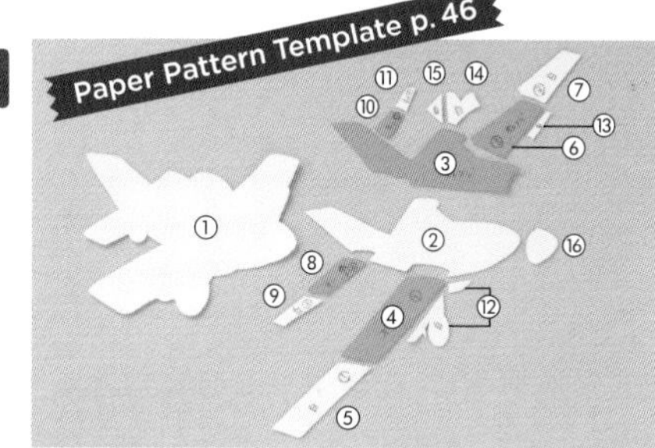

Create the paper pattern templates out of a milk carton (① Outline, ② Fuselage - Whole, ③ Fuselage - Orange Part of Pattern, ④ Right Front Wing 1, ⑤ Right Front Wing 2, ⑥ Left Front Wing 1, ⑦ Left Front Wing 2, ⑧ Right Back Wing 1, ⑨ Right Back Wing 2, ⑩ Left Back Wing 1, ⑪ Left Back Wing 2, ⑫ Right Front Wing Parts 2, ⑬ Left Front Wing Parts 2, ⑭ Face, ⑮ Window, ⑯ Nose).

Note: To make things easier to understand, Wing 1 is orange and Wing 2 is White.

2 Place paper template ① on the ham and cut around it. Place paper template ② on the cheese slice, cut around it, and place it on the outline.

3 Please paper templates ③, ④, ⑥, ⑧, and ⑩ on the ketchup omelette sheet, cut around them, and place them on **2**.

4 Place paper templates ⑤, ⑦, ⑨, ⑪, ⑫, ⑬, ⑭, ⑮, and ⑯ on the cheese slice, cut around them, and place them on **3**.

5 Trace the eyes, nose, mouth, eyebrows, patterns on the body, and pattern on the wings onto the baking paper, cut the shapes out of the nori sheet, and glue them on the body. Cut a thin and long strip of ketchup omelette sheet and place it in front of the tail fin as the antenna. Cut a small piece off the cheese slice for the back leg and place it above the back tire.

6 Pack half of the bento box with rice, fill in the open area with the side dishes and vegetables, and place **5** on top of the rice. Cut a thin slice off the broccoli stem, use the curve of a heart-shaped cutter to punch out two crescent shapes to use as the propeller, and place them next to the nose. If you don't have a heart-shaped cutter, trace the shape onto the baking paper and use that to cut the propellers from the nori sheet.

Lightning McQueen

Start your engines!

95

BENTO MENU

- Carrot and bean meat roll ▸p.88
- Mitsuba and shirasu omelette ▸p.91
- Lotus root dressed with cod roe ▸p.94
- **Ham and cheese license plate** (cheddar cheese cut out in the shape of numbers, placed on top of a piece of ham punched out with a flower-shaped cutter)
- **Rice** (square nori sheets placed on the rice in a checker pattern)
- **Pick-skewered edamame, broccoli, lettuce**

INGREDIENTS

Ham	1 slice
Red part (skin) **of the imitation crab**	2 sticks
Cheese slice	small amount
Snow peas in the pod (boiled in salted water)	small amount
Nori sheet	as needed

RECIPE

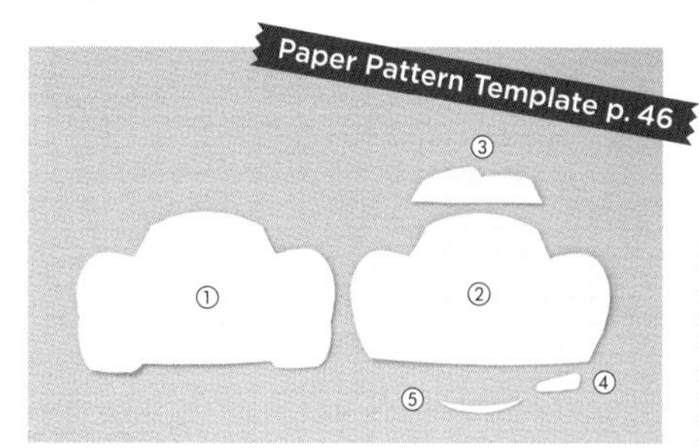

1 Create the paper pattern templates out of a milk carton (① Outline, ② Body, ③ Around the Eyes, ④ Lights, ⑤ Teeth).

2 Place paper template ① on the ham and cut around it.

3 Place the imitation crab on a piece of baking paper and place paper template ② on top of the imitation crab to cut out the body shape.

ATTENTION! Placing the imitation crab on baking paper will make it a lot easier to cut it with a pair of scissors.

4 Remove the imitation crab from **3** from the baking paper and place it on the ham from **2**.

5 Place paper template ③ on the cheese slice, cut around it, and place the cheese onto **4**.

6 Place paper template ④ on the cheese slice, create two of them by cutting around the template, and place them on **5**. (Flip one light over to use as the opposite light.)

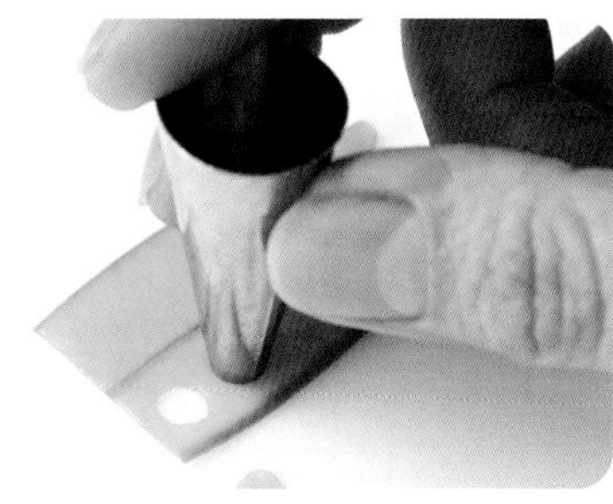

7 Use a piping tip to punch out round pieces from the snow peas and place them on **3** around the eyes.

8 Trace the pupils, mouth, and tires on a piece of baking paper. Place it over a nori sheet to cut out the shapes and glue them onto the body.

9 Place paper template ⑤ on the cheese slice. Cut around it and place the cheese piece on the mouth.

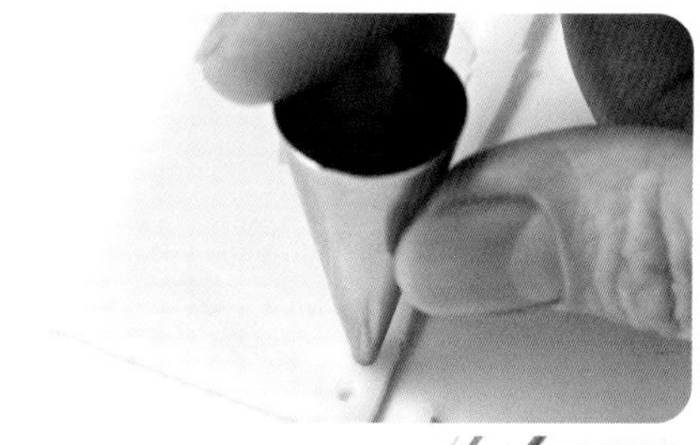

10 Use a piping tip to punch out the lights in the eyes from the cheese slice and place them on the pupils.

11 Pack half of the bento box with rice and place the square nori sheets on top of it in a checker pattern. Fill the open area with the side dishes and vegetables, and place **10** on top of the rice.

BENTO MENU

Grilled salmon wrapped in nori ▸p. 89

Simmered pumpkin ▸p. 91

Sautéed spinach with sakura shrimp ▸p. 93

Potato salad in a cherry tomato cup ▸p. 93

Carrot car (punch out a carrot using a car-shaped cutter, place windows and wheels made of cheese on it, and cut the tires out of the nori sheet)

Sausage star, broccoli, lettuce, rice

INGREDIENTS

- **Ham** ············ 1 slice
- **Satsuma-age** (deep-fried) fish cake* ············ 1 slice
- **Nori sheet** ············ as needed
- **Snow peas** (boiled in salted water) ····· small amount
- **Thinly sliced carrot** (boiled in salted water) ····· small amount

**Satsuma-age* is deep-fried fish cake. You can find it in Japanese and Asian supermarkets. Other deep-fried fish cakes, such as tempura, *odeng*, and *eomuk*, can replace satsuma-age as well. However, when using these replacement fish cakes, please make sure that the surface is golden brown without other colors, and the size is big enough to cut out the character. This recipe will use the inner white side of the fish cake to make some parts of the character, so if your replacement fish cake is not thick enough to be sliced in half or has nonwhite inner fillings, you can use a cheese slice to make the white parts instead.

CARS **The cheerful rickety tow truck!**

Mater

RECIPE

1 Paper Pattern Template p. 46

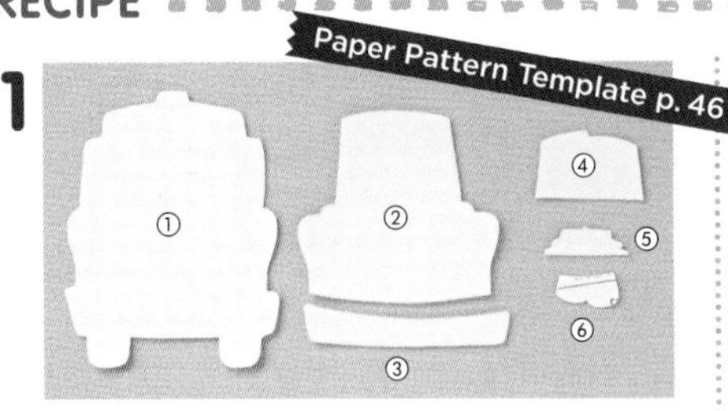

Create the paper pattern templates out of a milk carton (① Outline, ② Body, ③ Bumper, ④ Around the Eyes, ⑤ Nose, ⑥ Teeth).

ATTENTION! The body will be placed on the outline, so the outline should be a little larger than the actual paper template.

2 Place paper template ① on the ham and cut around it.

3 Slice the satsuma-age in half so you have two equal pieces. Then put paper templates ② and ③ on one piece (one half) of the satsuma-age. Cut around them and place both shapes on **2**.

4 Trace the bars of the side mirrors and the tires on a piece of baking paper. Place it over a nori sheet to cut the shapes out, and glue the parts onto the body.

5 Slice the remaining satsuma-age in half crosswise (from side to side, not top to bottom), place paper templates ④ and ⑤ on it, and cut around the templates. Punch out the right and left lights with a round piping tip from the remaining satsuma-age (the white part) and place them on the body.

6 Place paper template ⑥ on the satsuma-age (brown part) and cut around it. Cut the remaining satsuma-age (brown part) into small and large square pieces and place them as the mirrors and other decorative pieces on the body.

7 Punch the eyes out of the snow peas with a round piping tip and place onto the face.

8 Trace the pupils, pattern around the nose, mouth, and pattern on the left light onto baking paper, place it over a nori sheet to cut the shapes out, and glue them onto the body.

9 Punch the lights in the eyes out from the satsuma-age (white part) with a round piping tip and place them on the pupils.

10 Cut a square lamp shape out of the carrot, and place it on the head.

11 Pack half of the bento box with rice, fill the open area with the side dishes and vegetables, and place **10** on top.

MONSTERS, INC. **Monster friend goals!**

Sulley & Mike

BENTO MENU

- Grilled salmon wrapped in nori ▶p.89
- Simmered chikuwa fish cake and vegetables ▶p.91
- Mitsuba and shirasu omelette ▶p.91
- Potato salad in a cherry tomato cup ▶p.93
- Broccoli, snap pea pods, lettuce

INGREDIENTS

SULLEY

- **Rice** ···· 1.8 oz./50 g
- **Japanese basil rice seasoning** (use a mortar to powderize) ···· ¼ teaspoon
- **Cheese slice** ···· ¼ slice
- **Nori sheet** ···· as needed
- **Frankfurter or sausage** (0.6 inch of each end) ···· 1 sausage
- **Deep-fried pasta** ···· as needed

MIKE

- **Rice** ···· 1.8 oz./50 g
- **Edamame** (remove the thin skin and grind with a mortar) ···· 10 beans
- **Cheese slice** ···· ¼ slice
- **Nori sheet** ···· as needed
- **Snap peas** (boiled in salted water) ···· 1 pod
- **Deep-fried pasta** ···· as needed
- **Broccoli stem** (boiled in salted water) ···· 2 slices

RECIPE

Paper Pattern Template p. 47

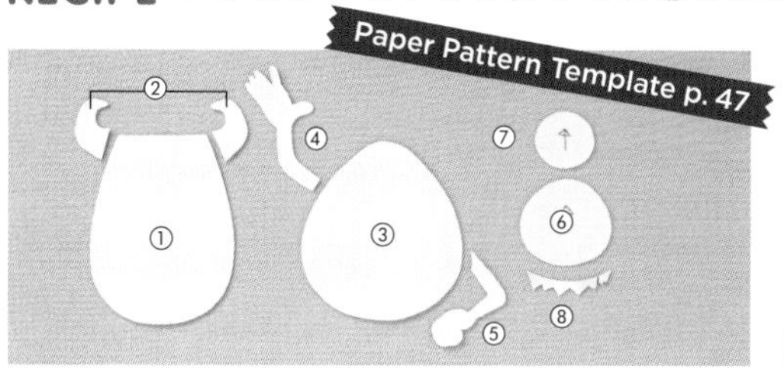

Create the paper pattern templates out of a milk carton (① Sulley's Face, ② Sulley's Horns, ③ Mike's Face, ④ Mike's Right Hand, ⑤ Mike's Left Hand, ⑥ Mike's Eye, ⑦ Mike's Pupil, ⑧ Mike's Teeth).

SULLEY

1. Sprinkle the Japanese basil rice seasoning onto the rice and mix it thoroughly. Lightly mold the rice into the shape of paper template ① and pack it into the bento box along with the other side dishes and vegetables.
2. Punch the eyes out from the cheese slice with a round piping tip and place them on the face.
3. Trace the eyebrows, pupils, nose, and mouth on a piece of baking paper. Place it over the nori sheet to cut the shapes out and glue them onto the face.
4. Punch the lights of the eyes out of the cheese slice using a round piping tip and place them on the pupils. Cut the cheese into triangles and place them on the mouth as teeth.
5. Slice the frankfurter or sausage in half and place paper template ② on it. Cut around the template to create the horns and attach them onto the head with deep-fried pasta.

MIKE

1. Mix the rice with ground edamame and a little bit of salt evenly. Lightly mold the rice into the shape of paper template ③. Pack it into the bento box next to Sulley's face.
2. Place paper template ⑥ on the cheese slice. Cut around it with a toothpick and place it on the face.
3. Trace the mouth on the baking paper, place it over the nori sheet to cut the shape out, and glue it onto the face.
4. Cut 0.2 inches off the edge of both sides of the snap peas to create the horns and attach them onto the top of the head with pieces of deep-fried pasta.
5. Place paper template ⑦ on the remaining snap peas. Cut around it and place it on the eye.
6. Punch out the light in the eye from the cheese slice with a round piping tip and place it on the pupil.
7. Place paper template ⑧ on the cheese slice and cut around it using a toothpick. Create triangles for the lower teeth and place them in the mouth.
8. Place paper templates ④ and ⑤ on the broccoli stem, cut around them to make the hands, and attach them onto the rice ball with deep-fried pasta.

BENTO MENU

- Salmon stir-fried in sweet vinegar ▸p.90
- Cabbage and carrot dressed with salted kelp ▸p.92
- **Badge** (cut a star-shaped piece of cheddar cheese, add a round white cheese slice on top, and place a star-shaped nori sheet on top of that)
- Little smokie flower, cherry tomato, broccoli, lettuce

INGREDIENTS

Rice	3.5 oz./100 g
Salted cod roe rice seasoning*	as needed
Seasoned deep-fried tofu pouch**	1 slice
Nori sheet	as needed
White cheese slice	small amount
Ham	1 slice
Deep-fried pasta	as needed

*You can usually find salted cod roe rice seasoning in Japanese and Asian supermarkets. It's usually labeled as "mentaiko furikake." You can use a little peanut powder with salt to replace it.

**You can also usually find seasoned deep-fried tofu pouches in Japanese and Asian supermarkets. It's called "inari age" for making inari sushi.

TOY STORY **Biggest, bestest hat ever!**

Woody

RECIPE

1 Paper Pattern Template p. 47

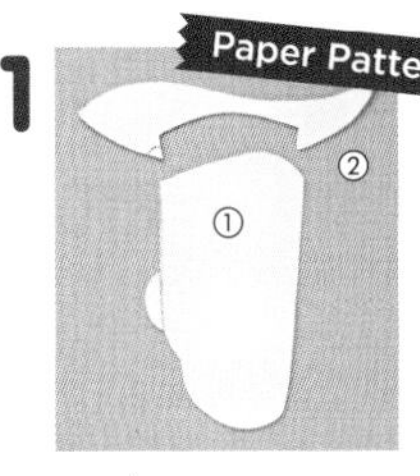

Create the paper pattern templates out of a milk carton (① Outline of Face, ② Brim).

2 Mix salted cod roe rice seasoning with rice evenly. Take a small amount and shape it into the ear.

3 Lightly mold the remaining rice into the shape of paper template ①.

4 Cut the flavored deep-fried tofu pouch into a long strip, wrap it around the top of **3**, and pack it into the bento box along with other side dishes and vegetables.

5 Trace the ribbon of the hat, hair, eyebrows, nose, and mouth on a piece of baking paper. Place it over the nori sheet to cut out the shapes and glue them onto the face.

6 Use a round piping tip to punch the eyes out of the cheese slice and place them on the face.

7 Cut out round pupils from the nori sheet and glue them onto the eyes from **6**.

8 Attach the ear from **2**.

9 Place paper template ② on the ham and deep-fried tofu pouch. Cut around the template, place the tofu pouch on the ham, and attach them to the rice ball with a piece of deep-fried pasta.

ATTENTION! The tofu pouch for the brim of the hat is unstable when used on its own, so add some thickness to it by placing it on top of a layer of ham.

TOY STORY **The cowgirl that everyone loves!**

Jessie

BENTO MENU

Chicken and sweet potato stir-fry ▸p.88

Pumpkin dressed with powdered cheese ▸p.91

Badge (cut the red part of the imitation crab into a heart shape and place it on a star-shaped cheese slice)

Japanese omelette, carrot heart, snap peas, cherry tomato, broccoli, lettuce, rice

INGREDIENTS

Ingredient	Amount
Ham	1 slice
Red part of the imitation crab	2 sticks
White part of the imitation crab	small amount
Chicken or turkey breast	½ slice
Thinly sliced kamaboko fish cake	1 slice
Dark-pink soft salami	small amount
Thin omelette sheet	small amount
Nori sheet	as needed

RECIPE

1. Create the paper pattern templates out of a milk carton (① Outline, ② Hat, ③ Brim, ④ Face with Neck, ⑤ Clothes, ⑥ Front Hair, ⑦ Face without Front Hair, ⑧ Back Hair, ⑨ Collar, ⑩ Ribbon).
2. Place paper template ① on the ham and cut around it.
3. Place the red part of the imitation crab on the baking paper. Place paper template ② over it and cut the shape out. Also place paper template ③ on the red part and cut around it. Remove the baking paper from the back of both pieces and place them on **2**.
4. Cut a long, thin strip from the white part of the imitation crab to create the ribbon for the hat and place it on **3**.
5. Place paper templates ④ and ⑦ on the chicken or turkey breast and cut around both of them. Place the face piece without front hair on top of the face piece with neck and then put both of them on **4**.
6. Place paper template ⑤ on the thin slice of fish cake and cut around it. Use a round piping tip to punch the eyes out and place them on the face.
7. Place paper templates ⑥ and ⑧ on the dark-pink soft salami and cut around them. Use a straw to punch out a circle from the remaining salami, and move the straw slightly to punch through that circle to create the mouth. Place all the pieces on the face.
8. Cut a thin strip off from the red part of the imitation crab to create the eyebrows and place them above the eyes.
9. Place paper templates ⑨ and ⑩ on the thin omelette sheet, cut around them, and place them on the body.
10. Trace the pupils and nose on a piece of baking paper. Place it over a nori sheet to cut the shapes out, and then glue them onto the face.
11. Pack half of the bento box with rice. Fill the open area with the side dishes and vegetables, and place **10** on top of the rice half.

TOY STORY **The stars and planets make it look like he's in space!**

Buzz Lightyear

BENTO MENU

Colorful sweet and sour chicken ▸p. 88

Planet (punch out a circle with a round cutter, then glue nori letters and cheese circles punched out with a small cutter to it, followed by a crescent-shaped snow pea on top)

Deep-fried sweet potato, pick-skewered edamame, boiled egg, broccoli, lettuce

INGREDIENTS

- **Rice** ··· 3.5 oz./100 g
- **Japanese basil rice seasoning*** (use a mortar to grind it) ··· roughly ½ teaspoon
- **Chicken or turkey breast** ··· 1 slice
- **Deep-fried pasta** ··· as needed
- **Cheese slice** ··· small amount
- **Nori sheet** ··· as needed

*You can find Japanese basil rice seasoning in Asian supermarkets and some general supermarkets. Usually it is labeled as "shiso fumi furikake." If you can't find this seasoning, you can replace ⅕ of the rice with black rice to make the rice mixture purple.

RECIPE

Paper Pattern Template p. 47

1

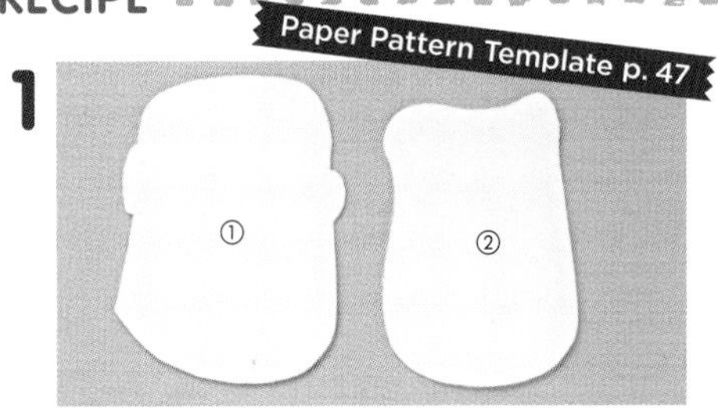

Create the paper pattern templates out of a milk carton (① Outline, ② Face).

2 Lightly mold the rice into the shape of paper template ①.

3 Sprinkle the Japanese basil rice seasoning on the surface of **2** and pack it into the bento box along with the other side dishes and vegetables.

4 Place paper template ② on the chicken or turkey breast. Cut around it and attach it onto the rice ball with a piece of deep-fried pasta.

5 Punch out the eyes from the cheese slice using a round piping tip and place them on the face.

6 Trace the eyebrows, pupils, nose, and mouth on a piece of baking paper. Place it over a nori sheet to cut the shapes out and glue them onto the face.

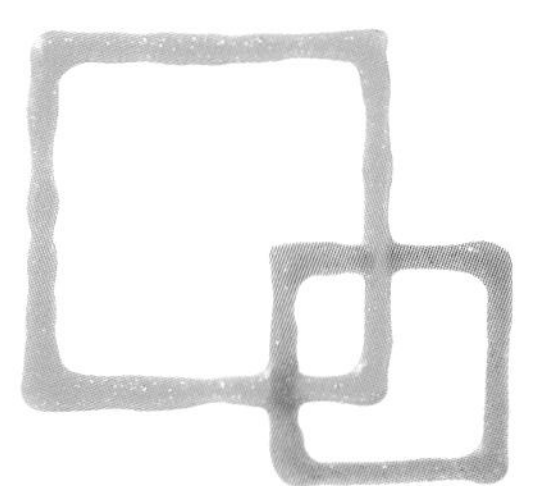

YOU'LL USE THESE A LOT!

CHARACTER PAPER TEMPLATE ILLUSTRATIONS

Photocopy these templates onto a piece of paper and enlarge or shrink them to the desired size. Character expressions may vary based on the difficulty of the bento recipe.

Goofy
p. 20
Chip & Dale
p. 21
Winnie the Pooh
p. 25
Winnie the Pooh
p. 22
Piglet
p. 23
Tigger
p. 25

Anna
p. 28
Elsa
p. 28
Olaf
p. 29
Oswald
p. 30
Lucky
p. 31

Stitch
p. 32
Nemo
p. 33
Baymax
p. 34
Dusty
p. 35
Mater
p. 38
Lightning McQueen
p. 37

Sulley & Mike
p. 39
Woody
p. 40
Jessie
p. 41
BUZZ
Buzz Lightyear
p. 42

MICKEY MOUSE & FRIENDS **A charming Mickey and Minnie bento!**

Mickey & Minnie

BENTO MENU

- Asparagus bacon roll ▸p. 91
- Pumpkin croquette with almond batter ▸p. 92
- Star-marked quail egg (punch out the surface of the quail egg with a star-shaped cutter and fill it with a carrot piece punched out with the same cutter; you can use a mozzarella cheese ball to replace the quail egg if you are unable to find one)
- Soft salami flower, snap peas, broccoli, lettuce

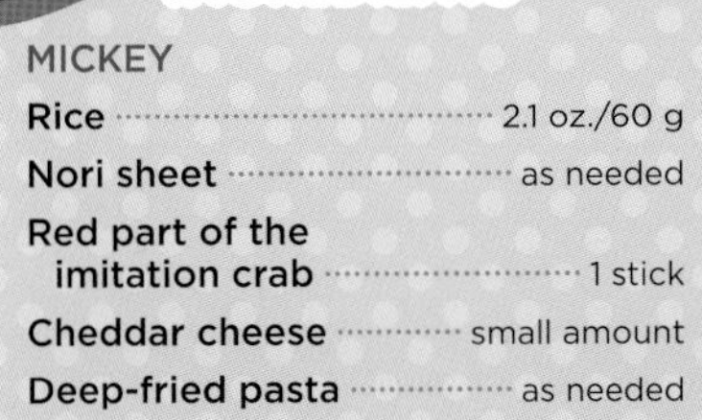

INGREDIENTS

MICKEY

- **Rice** ..... 2.1 oz./60 g
- **Nori sheet** ..... as needed
- **Red part of the imitation crab** ..... 1 stick
- **Cheddar cheese** ..... small amount
- **Deep-fried pasta** ..... as needed

MINNIE

- **Rice** ..... 2.1 oz./60 g
- **Nori sheet** ..... as needed
- **Red part of the imitation crab** ..... 1 stick
- **White part of the imitation crab** ..... small amount
- **Deep-fried pasta** ..... as needed

RECIPE

1 To make the Mickey rice ball, first separate 0.35 oz./10 g of rice into two equal portions and shape them into round balls as Mickey's ears. Then, shape the remaining 1.8 oz./50 g of rice into a patty shape to form Mickey's body.

2 Place the body rice ball at the center of a nori sheet, and cut a few lines from the edge of the nori toward the center to attach the nori to the curve of the rice ball.

3 Wrap two rice balls from **1** using the same method as **2**. Use cling wrap to cover the rice balls and let sit for few minutes while the nori softens.

4 Use tweezers to separate the red surface of the imitation crab from the white part. Wrap the red part onto the body rice ball from **3**.

5 Create the Minnie rice ball following steps **1–4** and pack them into the bento box along with the other side dishes and vegetables.

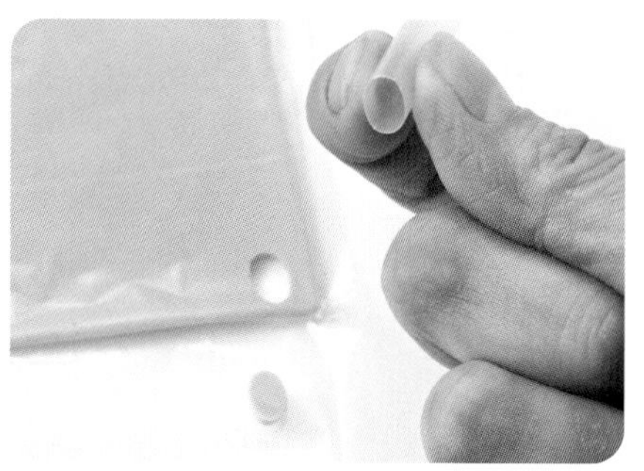

6 Squeeze a straw to punch out the buttons for the trousers from the cheddar cheese and place them on the body of Mickey's rice ball.

7 Use a straw to punch out the polka dots on the skirt from the white part of the imitation crab and place them on Minnie's body.

8 Use a toothpick to create two holes on the top of each rice ball.

ATTENTION! Creating holes for the ears with a toothpick will make it easier to stick the pasta into them.

9 Attach the ear rice balls by inserting deep-fried pasta into the holes created in **8**.

10 Create an additional hole on the top of the Minnie rice ball with a toothpick and stick a ribbon-shaped pick into it.

Minnie & Daisy

BENTO MENU

Sausage and bell pepper stir-fry ▸p. 89

Sautéed turnip with herbs ▸p. 91

Mickey Mouse mark quail egg* (punch three holes of different sizes into the surface of the quail egg)

Broccoli, lettuce

*If you can't find a quail egg, you can use a mozzarella ball (bocconcini) to replace it. Cut out the Mickey Mouse mark on the surface of mozzarella cheese, and then add in a cheddar cheese slice cut in the same shape.

INGREDIENTS

Rice	3.5 oz./100 g
Nori sheet	as needed
Cheese slice	1 slice
Cheddar cheese	small amount
Fish sausage (0.2 inch/5 mm slice)	2 slices
Deep-fried pasta	as needed
Ham	1 slice

RECIPE

1

Create the paper pattern templates out of a milk carton (① Minnie's Face, ② Minnie's Ear, ③ Daisy's Mouth).

Note: You can decide on the size of your paper template based on the size of your bento box.

2 Separate the rice into two 1.8 oz./50 g portions and shape them into two round patties.

3 Wrap one of the rice balls with nori and cling wrap. Set it for few minutes to let the nori soften. Then pack both rice balls and the side dishes and vegetables into the bento box.

4 Place paper template ① on the cheese slice. Cut around it and place the cheese piece on the Minnie rice ball from **3**.

5 Place paper template ③ on the cheddar cheese, cut around it, and place the cheese piece on the Daisy rice ball from **3**.

6 Place paper template ② on the fish sausage and cut off two slices. Use the same paper template to cut off two pieces from the cheese slice and two pieces from the nori sheet. Place the the cheese slice on top of the sausage slice, and place the nori sheet on top of that.. Attach the ears to the top of Minnie's rice ball with deep-fried pasta.

7 Cut Minnie's eyes, nose, and mouth, and Daisy's eyes and mouth out of the nori sheet, and glue them onto the faces.

8 Cut the ham into two circles and fold them to create the frills of the bows. Wrap a long strip of ham down across the middle to create the ribbon. Stick deep-fried pasta into the ribbons and attach them to the top of both rice balls.

9 Use a round piping tip to punch out four round blushes from the remaining ham and place them on the faces.

 The snap pea hat looks so cute!

Goofy

BENTO MENU

Colorful sweet and sour chicken ▸p.88

Japanese omelette ▸p.91

Simmered chikuwa fish cake and vegetables ▸p.91

Broccoli, lettuce

INGREDIENTS

Rice	3.5 oz./100 g
Nori sheet	as needed
Salmon flakes	as needed
Cheese slice	¼ slice
Cheddar cheese	⅛ slice
Deep-fried pasta	as needed
Snap pea	½ pod

RECIPE

1

Create the paper pattern templates out of a milk carton (① Around the Eyes, ② Around the Nose).

Note: Choose the exact print size of your paper template based on the size of your bento box.

2 Mold the rice into a patty shape.

3 Wrap the upper half of **2** with nori and sprinkle the remaining half with salmon flakes. Wrap the rice ball in cling wrap. Once the nori is softened, pack it into the bento box along with the other side dishes and vegetables.

ATTENTION! The nori sheet and salmon flakes will not stick well to the rice if it is cold, so wrap the rice while it's still warm.

4 Place paper template ① on the cheese slice, cut around it with a toothpick, and place it on the rice ball.

5 Place paper template ② on the cheddar cheese. Cut around it with a toothpick and place it on the rice ball.

6 Cut the eye and nose out of the nori sheet and glue them onto the face.

7 Stack four sheets of nori together and cut out the shape of the ear.

8 Glue one of the ears from **7** onto the cheese slice. Cut around it with a toothpick and glue another ear on the back.

9 Create another ear using the procedure from **8** and attach both ears to the rice ball with deep-fried pasta. To keep the pasta mostly hidden, like in the photo, first stick the pasta into the rice ball and then attach the ear so it hangs off the pasta.

10

Cut the snap pea into a 0.2 inch/5 mm piece and a longer piece as shown in the picture. Stick the longer snap pea piece into the center of the shorter piece to form the hat.

11 Cut a strip of nori. Glue it onto **10** and attach it to the rice ball with deep-fried pasta.

WINNIE THE POOH **Cute pointy ears!**

Pooh & Piglet

BENTO MENU

Stuffed bell pepper ▸p. 89

Lotus root and imitation crab salad ▸p. 90

Quail egg bee (marinate the quail egg in liquid curry to dye it yellow, score one side of the egg and place a slice of heart-shaped fish cake in it, and use nori to make the eyes and the pattern of the bee)

Broccoli, snap peas, asparagus, cherry tomato, lettuce

INGREDIENTS

POOH

Rice .... 1.8 oz./50 g
Pumpkin (cooked in microwave) .... as needed
Red part of the imitation crab .... 1 stick
Corn .... 2 kernels
Deep-fried pasta .... as needed

PIGLET

Rice .... 1.8 oz./50 g
Plum sushi vinegar (red)* .... as needed
Dark-pink soft salami .... 1 slice

*Plum sushi vinegar can be found in some Japanese grocery stores and Asian supermarkets. It's labeled as "ume plum vinegar" or "red plum vinegar." You can replace it with red wine vinegar, which has a brighter red color. Add a bit of sugar to adjust the taste if it's too sour.

RECIPE

POOH

1 Mix 1.8 oz./50 g of rice with mashed pumpkin and add a little salt to taste. Mold the rice ball into the shape of a patty.

2 Wrap the red part of the imitation crab around **1** and pack it into the bento box with the other side dishes and vegetables.

3 Attach the corn kernels to the top of the rice ball from **2** with deep-fried pasta.

PIGLET

1 Mix plum sushi vinegar with rice and mold it into a drum shape.

2 Slice the soft salami into long, thin strips and wrap them onto **1**. Place it next to Pooh.

3 Cut the remaining soft salami in the shape of Piglet's ears. Create a slit on the top of the rice ball with a knife and stick the salami in.

 His big ears are so charming!

Dumbo

BENTO MENU

- Mayo-teriyaki chicken ▸p. 88
- Simmered tri-color veggies ▸p. 93
- Japanese omelette ▸p. 91
- Star-marked quail egg (punch out the surface of the quail egg with a star-shaped cutter and stuff it with a carrot cut by the same cutter; if you can't find quail egg, use a mozzarella cheese ball as a substitute)
- Cherry tomato, boiled asparagus, lettuce

INGREDIENTS

- Rice .... 3.5 oz./100 g
- Ground black sesame .... ½ teaspoon
- Imitation crab ...... ⅔ stick
- Ham .... 1 slice
- Nori sheet .... as needed
- Thin omelette sheet .... small amount
- Deep-fried pasta .... as needed

RECIPE

1 Mix the ground black sesame and a little salt into the rice until even. Separate rice into four portions: face (2.7 oz./77 g), two ears (0.35 oz./10 g), and one nose (0.1 oz./3 g). Mold each part into shape.

ATTENTION! The rice balls for the ears should be large and flat. Place them on top of the side dishes and vegetables when packing them into the bento box.

2 Cut the imitation crab in half lengthwise, so you can see the jagged cross section.

3 Pack **1**, **2**, and the side dishes and vegetables into the bento box.

ATTENTION! Pack the rice balls in this order: 1) face rice ball → 2) side dishes and vegetables → 3) ear rice balls → 4) imitation crab → 5) nose rice ball.

4 Cut out two ears from the ham and place them on the ear rice ball.

5 Cut the eyes, lines of the nose, and lines on the forehead out of the nori sheet and glue them onto the face rice ball.

6 Punch out two slices of blush from the remaining ham with an oval cutter and place them onto the face.

7 Cut the thin omelette sheet in the shape of a hat. Place it on the ham, cut around it, and attach it on the top of the head using deep-fried pasta.

BEAUTY AND THE BEAST **Adorn Belle's gown with Mrs. Potts and Chip!**

Mrs. Potts & Chip

BENTO MENU

Sautéed carrot and burdock ▸p. 92

Ham rose (recipe on facing page)

Cherry tomato, broccoli, snap peas, lettuce, gomoku rice (also known as "mixed rice")

INGREDIENTS

Thin omelette sheet	½ slice
Cheese slice	1 slice
Cheddar cheese	small amount
Thinly sliced carrots (boiled in salted water)	1 slice

RECIPE

HAM ROSE

1. Cut the ham (loin or soft salami is fine) into quarters.
2. Hold one of the ham quarters with the center of the ham pointing down. Fold ⅓ of the top ham edge over and roll the ham as shown in the picture.
3. Fold the remaining ham in the same manner and wrap it around the rolled ham. After wrapping all the ham, fix the ham together with a piece of deep-fried pasta.

1 Create the paper pattern templates out of a milk carton (① Chip, ② Mrs. Potts).

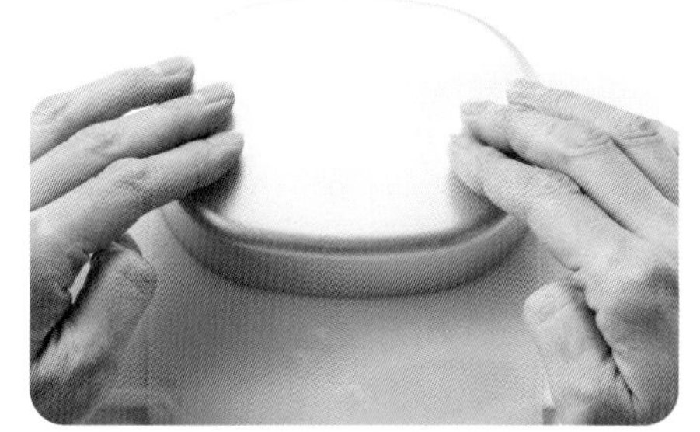

2 Use the bento box as a mold and press it onto the omelette sheet to cut out a shape that can cover half of the bento box.

3 Pack the bento box with the mixed rice, side dishes, and vegetables and place the thin omelette sheet from **2** onto the rice.

4 Cut the cheese slice into six long and thin triangles.

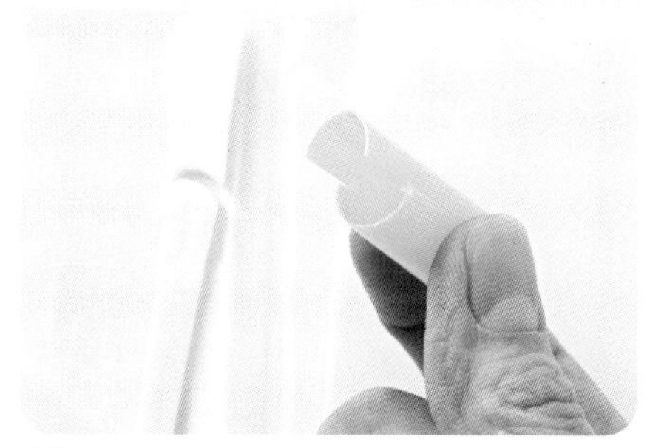

5 Cut a straw in half to form a semicircular edge. Use the half straw to create a curved edge on the cheese pieces from **4** on the wider side.

6 Place the six triangles from **5** on the omelette sheet.

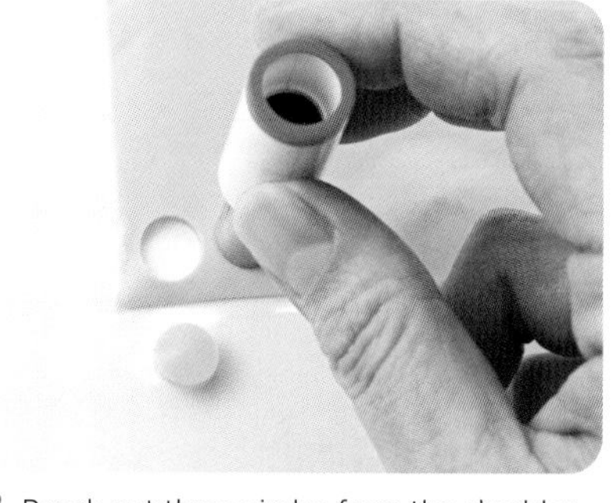

7 Punch out three circles from the cheddar cheese using a round cutter and place them on the omelette sheet.

8 Place paper templates ① and ② on the carrot, cut around them, and place the carrot cutouts on the thin omelette sheet with mayonnaise.

SNOW WHITE AND THE SEVEN DWARFS

Look at all the apples! This bento will make you feel like you're inside an orchard!

Snow White

BENTO MENU

- **Stuffed bell pepper** ▸p.89
- **Sautéed carrot** ▸p.93
- **Apple wrapped in an omelette sheet** (cut the imitation crab in half, wrap it with a thin omelette sheet, and place a leaf-shaped snap pea and black sesame on it)
- **Cheese bird** (place the paper template on the cheese slice and cut around it with a toothpick)
- **Cherry tomato, broccoli, snap pea, lettuce**

INGREDIENTS

APPLE RICE BALL

- **Rice** ······ 1.8 oz./50 g
- **Tomato ketchup** ······ roughly 1 teaspoon
- **Snack kelp** ······ 1 slice
- **Snap peas** (boiled in salted water) ······ small amount

RIBBON RICE BALL

- **Rice** ······ 1.8 oz./50 g
- **Favorite rice ball filling** ······ as needed
- **Nori sheet** ······ as needed
- **Red part of the imitation crab** ······ 1 stick
- **Cheese slice** ······ small amount

RECIPE

APPLE RICE BALL

1 Mix ketchup and a pinch of salt with the rice. Microwave the rice for about 20 seconds to reduce the moisture in it. Mix again and form the rice into a round shape.

2 Cut a long, thin strip from the snack kelp and stick it into the rice ball from **1**.

3 Cut the snap pea into the shape of a leaf and stick it into the rice ball from **2**.

RIBBON RICE BALL

1 Fill the rice with any of your favorite fillings and mold it into the shape of a patty.

2 se a craft puncher to create a lace pattern in the nori sheet, wrap the nori around the rice ball from ①, and pack it into the bento box with other side dishes and vegetables.

3 Cut the red part of the imitation crab into a long, thin strip and wrap it around the rice ball from **2**.

4   

Cut the red part of the imitation crab into the shape of a ribbon and fold it in half. Create another one and place both on **3**.

5 Use a heart-shaped cutter to punch a heart out of the cheese slice and place the heart on the ribbon from **4**. If you don't have a heart-shaped cutter, use a knife.

6 Use a heart-shaped cutter to punch out a heart from the red part of the imitation crab and place it on top of the cheese heart from **5**.

 The most wonderful adventure!

Alice in Wonderland

BENTO MENU

Lotus root and imitation crab salad ▶p.90

Boiled egg, cherry tomato, broccoli, lettuce

INGREDIENTS

CHESHIRE CAT HAM

- **Dark-pink soft salami** ········ ½ slice
- **Cheese slice** ········ small amount
- **Nori sheet** ········ small amount

CARD SANDWICHES

- **Sandwich bread** ········ 2 slices
- **Chocolate cream** ········ small amount
- **Strawberry jam** ········ small amount

SALISBURY STEAK WATCH

- **Cheese slice** ········ 1 slice
- **Burger patty** ········ 1 patty
- **Nori sheet** ········ small amount

RECIPE

CHESHIRE CAT HAM

1 

Create the paper pattern template out of a milk carton (① Outline).

2 Place paper template ① on the soft salami and cut around it.

3 Cut the cheese slice in the shape of a crescent and place onto **2**.

4 Cut thin strips out of the nori sheet for the lines of the teeth and glue them onto **3**.

CARD SANDWICHES

1 Cut a slice of the sandwich bread into quarters and punch out the center using cutters (diamond, spade, heart, and club shapes). If you don't have a cutters, use a regular small knife to cut out the shapes.

2 Cut the other sandwich bread slices into quarters and spread chocolate cream on two of them and strawberry jam on the other two. Attach all the quarters of the bread to the bread from **1** to form the poker sandwich.

BURGER PATTY WATCH

1 Cut the cheese slice into a circle and place it on a round burger patty.

2 Cut the nori sheet into the hands of the watch and dials and glue onto **1**.

3 Stick the ring-shaped pick into the top of **2**.

Toy Story

Start your engines!

BENTO MENU

Salmon roll ▸p.90

Sautéed potato and corn ▸p.93

Marinated bell pepper and mushroom ▸p.93

Salted rice ball (tear pieces of the nori sheet and stick them onto the rice ball to create the cow pattern)

Carrot stars, asparagus, broccoli, lettuce

INGREDIENTS

MASHED EDAMAME LITTLE GREEN MEN

Edamame (boiled in salted water) ········ as needed

JESSIE'S HAT

Ham ········ ½ slice

Red part of the imitation crab ········ 1 stick

White part of the imitation crab ········ small amount

Snow peas (boiled in salted water) ········ small amount

Spaghetti (boiled in salted water) ········ 1 strand

Deep-fried pasta ········ as needed

WOODY'S HAT

Satsuma-age fish cake ········ 1 slice

Deep-fried pasta ········ as needed

Cheddar cheese ········ small amount

Nori sheet ········ small amount

Paper Pattern Template Examples

RECIPE

Create the paper pattern templates out of a milk carton (① Jessie's Hat, ② Woody's Hat, ③ Ribbon on Woody's Hat, ④ Little Green Men Face).

MASHED EDAMAME LITTLE GREEN MEN

1 Remove the thin skin from one edamame and separate the edamame into halves. Cut off the edge of each half with a straw to create the ears.

2 

Remove the thin skin from the remaining edamame and mash them in a mortar until they have a smooth texture.

3 Roll **2** into a ball and adjust its shape in accordance with paper template ④.

4 

Stick **1** into both ends of **3**.

5 Stick the green pick into the top of **4**.

JESSIE'S HAT

1 Place paper template ① on the ham and cut around it.

2 Place the red part of the imitation crab on baking paper, place paper template ① on it, and cut off the excess parts. Remove the baking paper and place it on **1**.

3 

Cut a thin strip off from the white part of the imitation crab and place it on **2**.

4 

Use a star-shaped cutter to punch out a star from the snow pea and place it on **3**.

5 

Place a small amount of mayonnaise on the boiled spaghetti and glue it onto the rice ball.

6 Attach **4** onto the rice ball using the deep-fried pasta.

WOODY'S HAT

1 

Place paper template ② on the satsuma-age fish cake. Cut around the template and attach the fish cake onto the rice ball with deep-fried pasta.

2 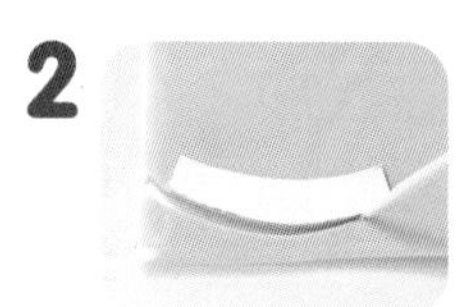

Place paper template ③ on the cheddar cheese and cut around it with a toothpick. Place it on **1**.

3 Cut the patterns of the ribbon out from the nori sheet and glue the pieces onto **2**.

4 

Punch a star out of the remaining cheddar cheese with a star-shaped cutter and place it on **3**.

BENTO MENU

- Salmon patty ▶p. 90
- Candied sweet potato ▶p. 92
- Marinated broccoli and cherry tomato ▶p. 93
- **Boiled egg planet** (glue a crescent-shaped carrot and circles from the red part of the imitation crab onto a half-cut boiled egg)
- Lettuce

INGREDIENTS

Rice ········· 3.5 oz./100 g
Japanese basil rice seasoning (use a mortar to pulverize) ········· ¼ teaspoon
Edamame (remove the thin skin and grind them with a mortar) ········· 10 beans
Nori sheet ········· as needed
Cheese slice ········· small amount
Snow peas (boiled in salted water) ········· 1 pod

TOY STORY **Friendly little aliens!**

Little Green Men

RECIPE

1 Separate the rice into two 1.8 oz./50 g portions. Mix Japanese basil rice seasoning with one portion of the rice and shape it like a patty.

2 Mix the mashed edamame thoroughly into the other portion of rice. Add some salt to taste and mold it into a patty shape.

3 Cut **1** and **2** in half with a kitchen knife, stick the two different halves of the rice balls together, and adjust its shape.

ATTENTION! Cut through the cling wrap around the rice ball with a wet kitchen knife to avoid ruining the shape.

4 Wrap a strip of nori around the center of the two rice balls that covers up the part where the two rice colors come together. Pack both rice balls into the bento box along with the other side dishes and vegetables.

5 Use a round piping tip to punch six circles out of the cheese slice and place three of them onto each rice ball as the eyes.

6 Cut the pupils and mouth out of the nori sheet and glue them onto the face.

7 Cut four ears out of the snow pea and stick them into the rice balls.

8 Stick green toothpicks into the top of the heads.

 That cap looks great on you! Pizza for lunch?

Mike

BENTO MENU

- Ham and cheese roll ▸p.89
- Scrambled egg with prawn and asparagus ▸p.90
- Sweet potato croquette ▸p.92
- Snap peas, lettuce

INGREDIENTS

MIKE

- **Rice** ..... 1.8 oz./50 g
- **Edamame** (remove the thin skin and grind them with a mortar) ..... 10 beans
- **Thinly sliced kamaboko fish cake** ..... 1 slice
- **Deep-fried pasta** ..... as needed
- **Snap peas** (boiled in salted water) ..... small amount
- **Nori sheet** ..... as needed
- **Pickled baby eggplant** ..... 1 eggplant

PIZZA

- **Rice** ..... 1.8 oz./50 g
- **Ham** ..... ¼ slice
- **Cheddar cheese** ..... ¼ slice
- **Cheese slice** ..... small amount
- **Red part of the imitation crab** ..... small amount
- **Snow peas** (boiled in salted water) ..... small amount
- **Nori sheet** ..... small amount
- **Deep-fried pasta** ..... as needed

RECIPE

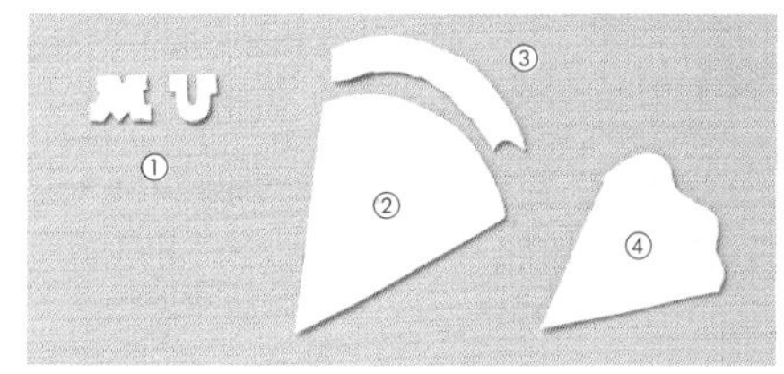

Create the paper pattern templates out of a milk carton (① Letters on the Cap, ② Pizza Outline, ③ Pizza Crust, ④ Pizza Cheese).

MIKE

1. Mix the mashed edamame thoroughly into the rice and add some salt to taste. Mold the rice into a patty shape and pack it into the bento box along with the other side dishes and vegetables.
2. Use a round piping tip or cutter to punch out the eye from the fish cake. Cut two small triangles from the remaining fish cake for the horns and attach them onto the rice ball from **1** using the deep-fried pasta.
3. Use a round piping tip to punch out the eye from a snap pea and place it on the fish cake.
4. Cut the pupil and mouth out of the nori sheet and glue them onto the face.
5. Cut the tip off from the pickled baby eggplant to create the cap and attach it onto the rice ball with a piece of deep-fried pasta.
6.  Place paper template ① on the fish cake, cut around it, and place the letters on the cap.
7. Cut the patterns of the cap out of the nori sheet and glue onto **6**.

ATTENTION! Glue the nori onto the fish cake. The nori will not be very clear if you stick it directly on the eggplant.

PIZZA

1. Mold the rice into a patty shape and place it next to Mike.
2. Place paper template ② on the ham and cut around it.
3. Place paper templates ② and ③ on the cheddar cheese and cut around it. Place the pizza crust on top of the pizza outline.
4. Place paper template ④ on the cheese slice, cut around it, and place the cheese cutout on **3**.
5. Use a round piping tip to punch out circles from the red part of the imitation crab and place them on **4**. Chop the remaining imitation crab and snow pea into small pieces and stick them onto **4** along with small bits of nori.
6. Attach **5** onto the rice ball from **1** using the deep-fried pasta.

BENTO MENU

Sausage and bell pepper stir-fry ▸p.89

German potato ▸p.93

Apple wrapped in omelette sheet
(cut the imitation crab in half, wrap it with a thin omelette sheet, place the leaf-shaped snap pea and deep-fried pasta between the omelette sheet and imitation crab, and place the black sesame seeds on the imitation crab, as pictured above)

Broccoli, cherry tomato, string bean, lettuce

INGREDIENTS

Rice	3.5 oz./100 g
Ham	1 slice
Nori sheet	as needed
Thinly sliced kamaboko fish cake	1 slice
Deep-fried pasta	as needed

THE ARISTOCATS

Marie

Her pink ribbon is her trademark!

RECIPE

1 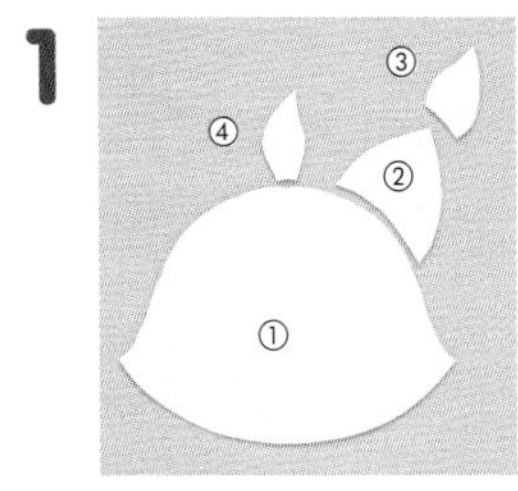

Create the paper pattern templates out of a milk carton (① Face, ② Ear, ③ Inside the Ear, ④ Fur).

2 Separate the rice into three portions: 2.8 oz./80 g and two portions of 0.35 oz./10 g. Use paper templates ① and ② to mold the 2.8 oz./80 g of rice into the shape of the face and two 0.35 oz./10 g portions into ears. Flip the template for the ear to make the opposite ear.

3 Pack **2** into the bento box along with the other side dishes and vegetables.

4 Place paper template ③ on the ham. Cut around it and place that piece onto the right ear. Then flip the template over to cut the inner ear of the left ear.

5 Cut the eyes, eyebrows, lines of the nose, mouth, and lines of the chin from a nori sheet and glue them onto the rice ball.

6 Punch the nose and inside of the mouth out of the ham with a straw and place them on the rice ball.

7 Place paper template ④ on the kamaboko fish cake. Cut around the paper template and attach the fish cake piece to the rice ball with deep-fried pasta.

8 Cut a circle out of the ham, and then fold the circles in half to create frills. Use a long, thin strip of ham to wrap the frills in the middle to create a ribbon. Stick the deep-fried pasta into the ribbon and attach it to the top of the head.

BENTO MENU

- **Broccoli meatball** ▸p.89
- **Sautéed lotus root** ▸p.93
- **Flower pattern quail egg*** (punch five holes into the surface of the egg with a squeezed straw)
- **Corn on the cob, broccoli, snap peas, cherry tomato, fruits** (mandarin orange, grape), **lettuce**

*If you can't find quail egg, use a mozzarella cheese ball (bocconcini) to replace it. Punch or cut out the holes and the cheddar cheese slices. Place the cheese slices into the holes.

INGREDIENTS

Rice ···· 3.5 oz./100 g
Pumpkin (cooked in microwave) ··· as needed
Deep-fried pasta ···· as needed
Cheese slice ···· 1 slice
Ham ···· ½ slice
Nori sheet ···· as needed
Carrot (boiled in salted water) ···· small amount
Cheddar cheese ···· small amount

BAMBI **The flower on the ear is so cute!**

Miss Bunny

RECIPE

1 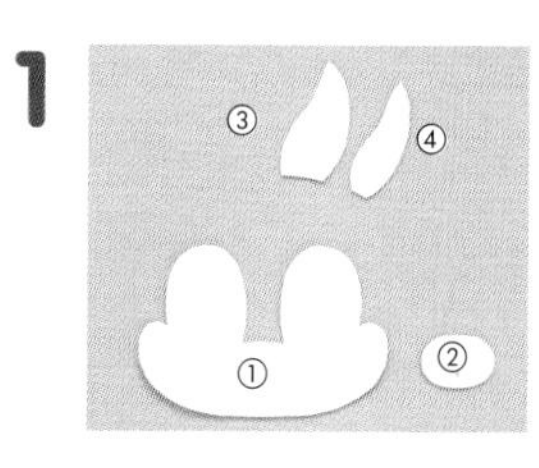

Create the paper pattern templates out of a milk carton (① Face, ② Snout, ③ Ear, ④ Inside the Ear).

2 Mix the rice with the mashed pumpkin and add a pinch of salt to taste. Mold 3.2 oz./90 g of the rice into an oval shape and pack it into the bento box along with the other side dishes and vegetables.

3 Separate the remaining 0.35 oz./10 g into two equal portions. Mold them into the shape of the ears using paper template ③. Flip one ear over for the opposite ear and attach both ears to the rice ball with deep-fried pasta.

4 Place paper templates ① and ② on the cheese slice. Cut around them and place them on the rice ball. First place the face, then the snout, and then the pink middle of the nose.

5 Place paper template ④ on the ham. Cut two slices out and place them on the ears (flip one over and use it for the inside of the opposite ear).

6 Punch three circles for the nose and cheeks out of the ham with a round piping tip and place them on the face.

7 Cut the pupils from the nori sheet and glue them onto the face.

8 Punch the lights in the eyes out from the cheese slice with a round piping tip and place them on the eyes.

9 Use a flower-shaped cutter to punch out a flower from the carrot slice. Use a round piping tip to cut out a circular cheddar cheese piece. Place the cheese on top of the carrot and attach the flower to the rice ball with a piece of deep-fried pasta.

Give it a try!
SILHOUETTE BENTO

MICKEY MOUSE & FRIENDS

Mickey & Minnie

Holding hands. ♪

BENTO MENU

Japanese fried chicken on a pick ▸p.88

Simmered potato and carrot (punch the center out with a Mickey Mouse cutter and swap the center pieces)

Fruits (kiwi, kyoho grape), **broccoli, lettuce, sandwich** (with your favorite filling)

INGREDIENTS

Nori sheet .... as needed
Ham .... 1 slice
Cheese slice .... 1 slice

RECIPE

1 Trace the illustration onto baking paper.

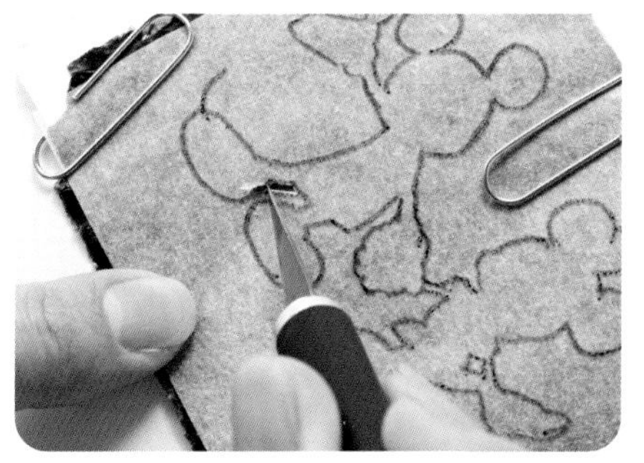

2 Place **1** on top of the nori sheet and cut out the silhouette with a garnishing knife.

ATTENTION! It will make the cutting easier if you place a milk carton underneath the nori sheet and fasten the baking paper and nori together with a paper clip.

3 Cut around the outline.

ATTENTION! Store the nori cutout properly so it won't get damp once it's cut.

4 Create a paper pattern template out of the milk carton.

5 Place the paper template on the ham and cut around it.

6 Punch holes into **5** to create the pattern.

7 Cut a circle out of the cheese slice with a round cutter and place it on **6**.

8 Glue the nori (silhouette) from **3** onto **7**. Pack the sandwiches, side dishes, and vegetables into the bento box and place the flower with the silhouette on the sandwich.

 Fly high into the sky with the balloon!

Winnie the Pooh

BENTO MENU

Chicken and sweet potato stir-fry ▶p. 88

Cabbage and carrot dressed with salted kelp ▶p. 92

Little smokies flowers (corn in the center), broccoli, snap peas, cherry tomato, lettuce, rice with seasoning

INGREDIENTS

Nori sheet ········ as needed
Thin omelette sheet ········ ½ sheet
Cheese slice ········ small amount

RECIPE

1. Trace the illustration onto baking paper.
2. Place **1** on top of the nori sheet and cut out the silhouette with a garnishing knife.

   ATTENTION! The string of the balloon is very thin and will easily break, so cut the string out separately.
3. Push the bento box onto the omelette sheet and cut it so that it is half the size of the bento box (see p. 55, step 2).
4. Pack the bento box with seasoned rice, side dishes, and vegetables and place the omelette sheet from **3** onto the rice.
5. Glue the nori (silhouette) from **2** onto the omelette sheet.
6. Decorate the bento with clouds cut out of cheese with a cloud-shaped cutter.

PETER PAN Is she casting a spell?

Tinker Bell

BENTO MENU

Carrot and pork patty ▸p.89

Broccoli and imitation crab dressed in mayonnaise ▸p.90

Sautéed carrot ▸p.93

Omelette sheet rose (recipe below), ham rose (recipe below), snap peas, lettuce, seasoned rice

INGREDIENTS

Nori sheet .... as needed
Cheese slice .... 1 slice
Ham .... 1 slice

RECIPE

1. Trace the illustration onto baking paper.
2. Place **1** on top of the nori sheet and cut the shape out with a garnishing knife.
3. Glue the nori (silhouette) from **2** onto the cheese slice and cut off the extra cheese around it with a toothpick.
4. Place **3** on top of the loin ham and cut off the extra ham with a knife.

THIN OMELETTE SHEET ROSE

1. Cut the omelette sheet in half, lengthwise, then take one piece of the omelette sheet and fold it in half, lengthwise.
2. Starting from the edge of the folded end of the omelette sheet, create incisions at 0.8 inch/2 cm, 0.2 inch/0.5 cm, 0.2 inch/0.5 cm, and 0.2 inch/0.5 cm. After that, create a 0.2 inch/0.5 cm incision every 0.6 inch/1.5 cm. Roll the omelette sheet and fasten it with deep-fried pasta.

ATTENTION! Use the remaining omelette sheet to create sparks of light to place around the character for a dreamy atmosphere.

HAM ROSE

1. Cut the ham (loin or soft salami is fine) into quarters.
2. 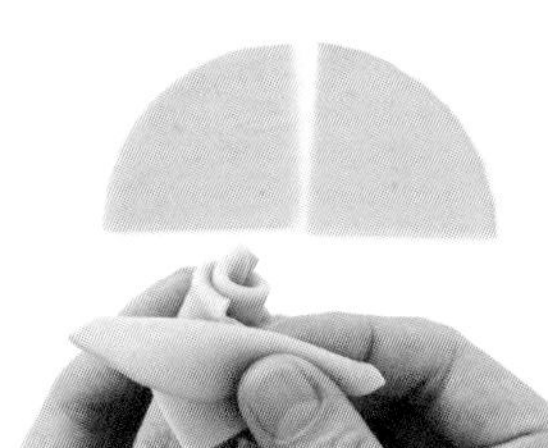

   The center of the ham should be downward. Fold ⅓ of the ham edge outward and roll the ham as pictured.
3. Fold the remaining ham in the same manner and wrap it around the rolled ham. After wrapping all the ham, fix together with deep-fried pasta.

Cinderella

Ride the carriage to the ball!

BENTO MENU

Meatball ▸p.89

Mitsuba and shirasu omelette ▸p.91

Simmered root vegetables ▸p.94

Fish sausage* rose, broccoli, lettuce, seasoned rice

*You can find fish sausages in Asian supermarkets or substitute a frankfurter.

INGREDIENTS

CINDERELLA

Nori sheet	as needed
Ham	1 slice
Cheese slice	1 slice

PUMPKIN CARRIAGE

Rice	0.7 oz./20 g
Pumpkin (cooked in microwave)	as needed
Cheddar cheese	small amount
Kelp (or nori)	small amount
Wagon wheel pasta	2 pieces

Paper Pattern Template Examples

RECIPE

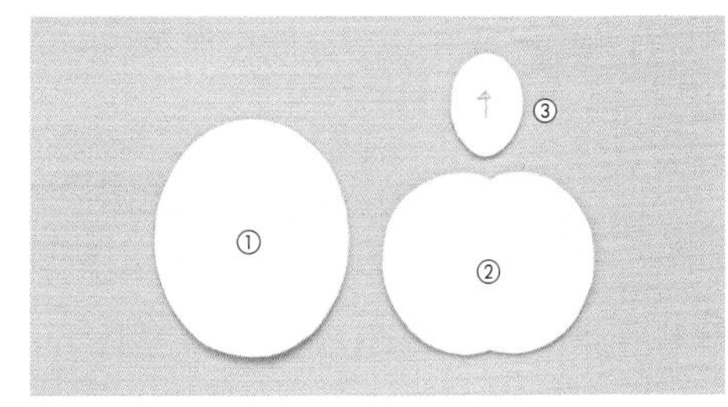

Create the paper pattern templates out of a milk carton (① Base for Cinderella, ② Body of Carriage, ③ Carriage Window).

CINDERELLA

1 Trace the illustration onto baking paper.

2 Place **1** on top of the nori sheet and cut the shape with a garnishing knife.

ATTENTION! There are no areas in the illustration that you need to hollow out, so you can also use scissors.

3

Punch a flower out of the ham with a flower-shaped cutter.

4

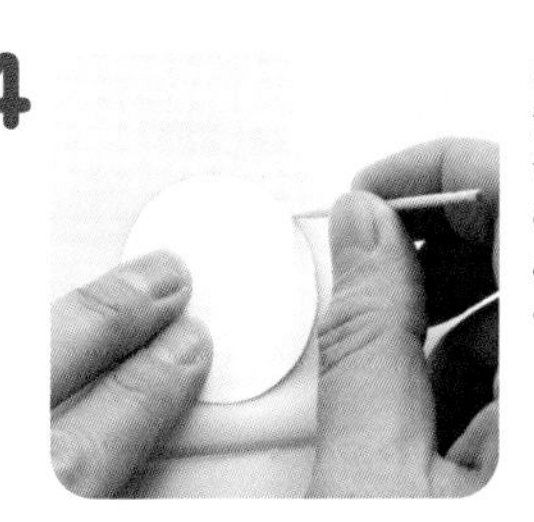

Place paper template ① on the cheese slice, cut around it, and place the circle on **3**.

5 Glue the nori (silhouette) from **2** onto **4**.

PUMPKIN CARRIAGE

1

Mix the rice with mashed pumpkin and add a little salt to taste.

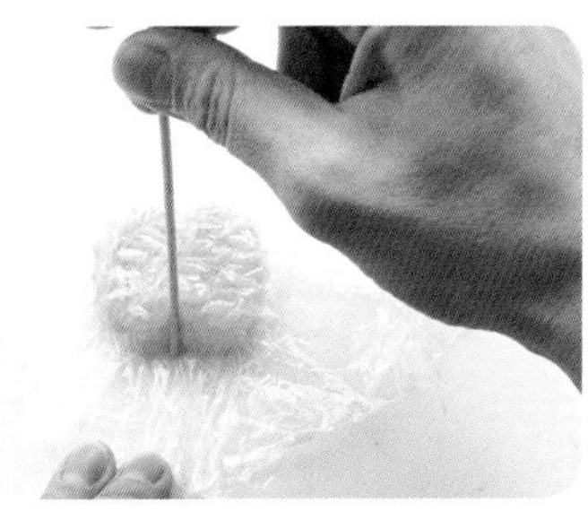

2 Lightly mold the rice into the shape of the carriage on paper template ② with a bamboo skewer or something similar. Pack the bento box with rice as shown below and place the carriage on top of the rice.

3 Place paper template ③ on the cheddar cheese. Cut around it and place the cheese piece on the carriage.

4 Use kelp or nori to create the pattern of the carriage and place it on the carriage.

5 Use a squeezed straw to punch out a piece of tear-shaped cheddar cheese and place it beneath the window.

6 Sprinkle rice seasoning onto the bottom of the rice and place the two pieces of boiled wagon wheel pasta underneath the carriage as the wheels.

TANGLED **Let down your hair!**

Rapunzel

BENTO MENU

- Flower pattern meat roll ▸p.88
- Sautéed turnip with herbs ▸p.91
- Japanese-style marinated mushrooms ▸p.92
- **Bale-shaped rice ball** (wrapped with a belt of ham and an omelette sheet)
- Fish sausage rose, purple sweet potato flowers, fish cake flower, carrot flower, broccoli, cherry tomato, lettuce

INGREDIENTS

Nori sheet ············ as needed
Ham ···························· 1 slice

Paper Pattern Template Examples

RECIPE

1. Trace the illustration onto baking paper.
2. Place **1** on top of the nori sheet and cut it out with a garnishing knife.
3. Cut the lantern pattern out of the ham and place it on one of the bale-shaped rice balls.
4. Glue the nori (silhouette) from **2** onto the other bale-shaped rice ball.

ATTENTION! Decorate the bento box by adding flowers of various colors.

THE LITTLE MERMAID **Under the sea!**

Ariel

BENTO MENU

Japanese omelette ▸p.91

Japanese-style marinated mushrooms ▸p.92

Salmon-stuffed lotus root ▸p.94

Carrot fish, bell pepper starfish, snap pea (to make sour "seaweed") cherry tomato, snap peas, lettuce, salted rice ball

INGREDIENTS

Nori sheet	as needed
Ham	2 slices
Cheddar cheese	½ slice
Cheese slice	1 slice

RECIPE

1. Trace the illustration onto baking paper.
2. Place **1** on top of the nori sheet and cut out the pieces using a garnishing knife.
3. 

Create the paper pattern template out of a milk carton (① Shell). Hollow out the shell patterns.

4. Place paper template ① on the ham and cut out two shell shapes (don't hollow out the shell patterns).
5. Use a toothpick to cut out the shell patterns from the cheddar cheese and place them on one of the ham shells from **4**.
6. Place paper template ① on the cheese slice, cut around it (hollow out the shell patterns too), and place it on the other ham shell from **4**.
7. Glue the nori (silhouette) from **2** onto **6**.

ATTENTION! Packing the food into a blue bento box will add an undersea vibe.

Fun Bento Recipes
FOR SPECIAL
EVENTS!

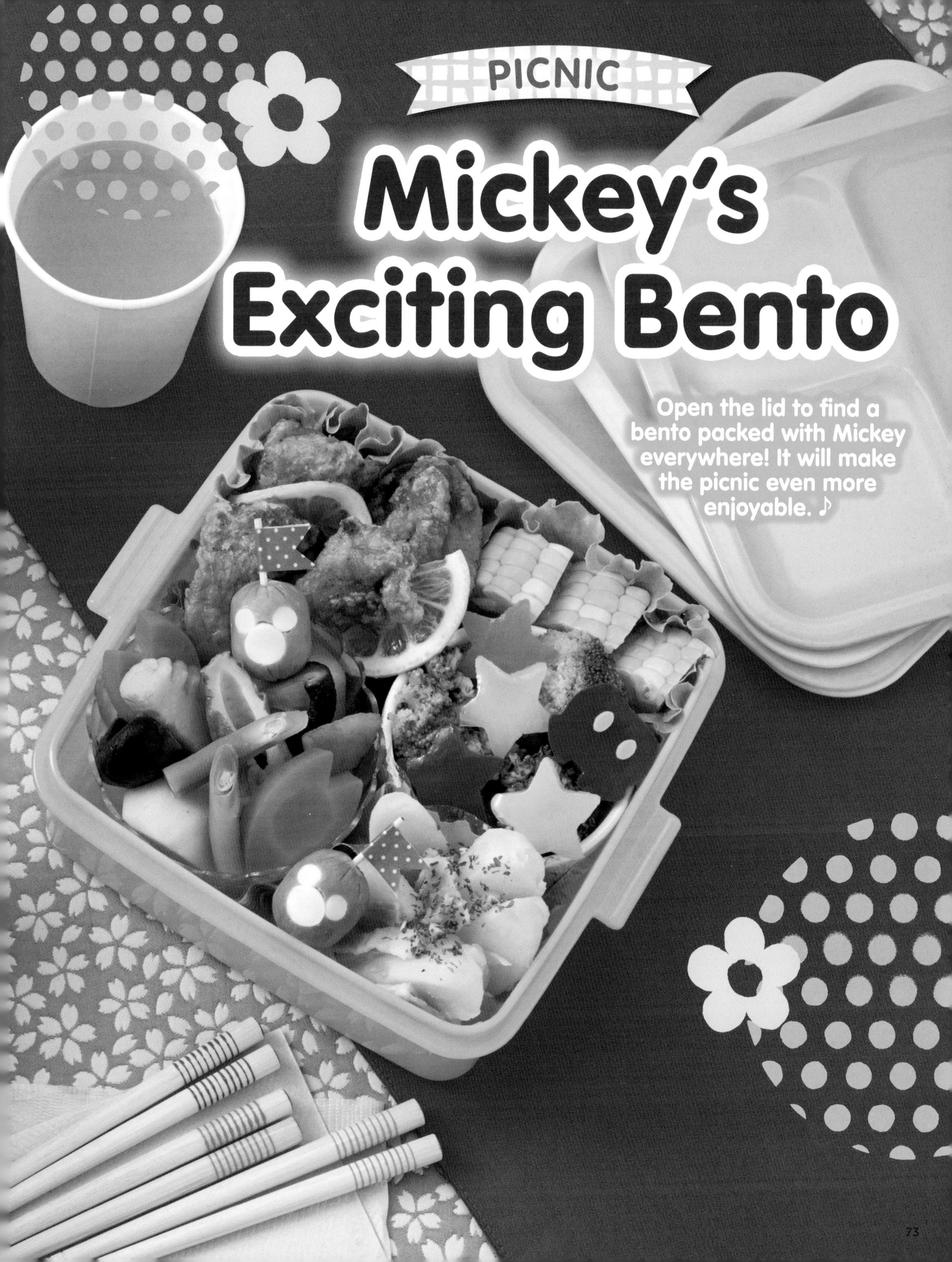
PICNIC
Mickey's Exciting Bento
Open the lid to find a bento packed with Mickey everywhere! It will make the picnic even more enjoyable. ♪

BENTO MENU

- Mickey tofu pouch sushi
- Mickey's hand pattern tofu pouch sushi
- Mickey thick roll
- Mickey logo sausages
- Mickey Mouse pants apple
- Japanese fried chicken ▶p.88
- German potato ▶p.93
- Marinated broccoli and bell pepper ▶p.93
- Simmered root vegetables ▶p.94
- **Fruits** (orange, apple, grape), **corn on the cob, parsley, lettuce**

INGREDIENTS

MICKEY TOFU POUCH SUSHI
(Amount for 1 sushi)

- **Sushi rice** .... 1.4 oz./40 g
- **Nori sheet** .... as needed
- **Red part of the imitation crab** .... 1 stick
- **Seasoned deep-fried tofu pouch** .... 1 slice
- **Black beans** (cooked) .... 2 beans
- **Deep-fried pasta** .... as needed
- **Cheddar cheese** .... small amount

MICKEY'S HAND PATTERN TOFU POUCH SUSHI
(Amount for 1 sushi)

- **Sushi rice** .... 1.4 oz./40 g
- **Seasoned deep-fried tofu pouch** .... 1 slice
- **Trefoil*** (boiled in salted water) 2
- **Thinly sliced hanpen fish cake**** (use the remaining hanpen from the Mickey Thick Roll and cut its thickness in half) .... small amount
- **Black sesame** .... 3 grains

*If you can't find trefoil, you can use a piece of scallion, leek, or spring onion.

**Hanpen fish cake is a type of Japanese fish cake made with fish and yams. You can find these in Japanese and Asian supermarkets. Alternatively, you can use some hard white cheese, such as Swiss cheese. But if you're substituting cheese, make sure the omelette isn't too hot or the cheese will melt.

RECIPE

MICKEY TOFU POUCH SUSHI

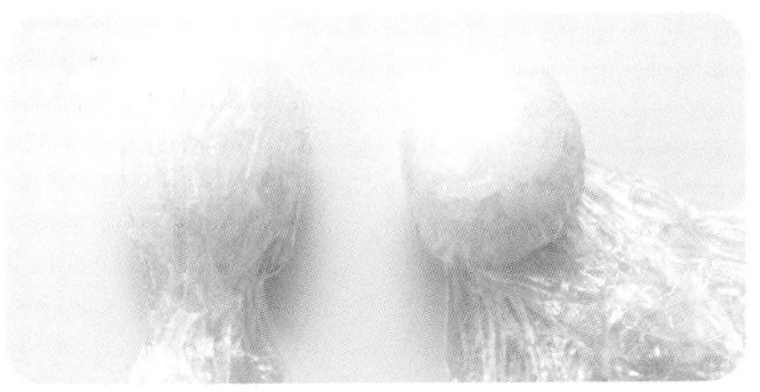

1 Separate the sushi rice into two 0.7 oz./20 g portions and shape them both into ovals.

2 Cover the surface of one rice ball with nori and wrap in cling wrap for 2–3 minutes until the nori is moist.

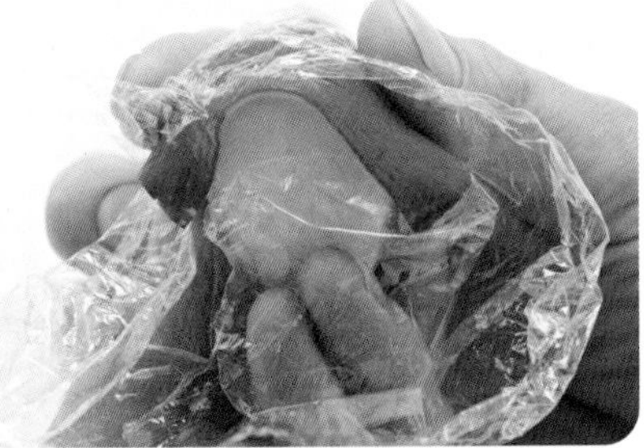

3 Cover the surface of the other rice ball with the red part of the imitation crab and wrap it in cling wrap for 2–3 minutes until the imitation crab is attached to the rice.

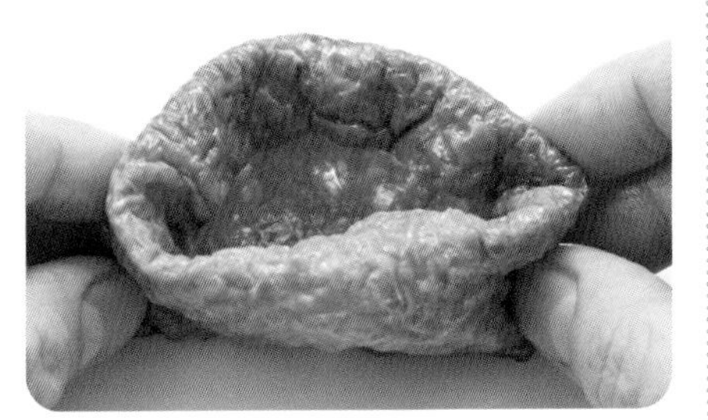

4 Fold around 0.4 inch/1 cm of the edge of the seasoned tofu pouch inside the pouch and open it up like a bag.

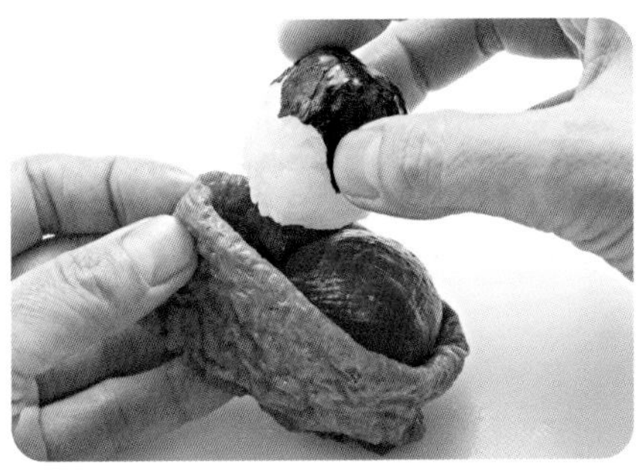

5 Place the rice balls from **2** and **3** into **4**.

6 Wrap black beans with nori and attach them to the nori-covered rice ball with deep-fried pasta.

7 Punch out two oval shapes from the cheddar cheese with a squeezed straw and place them on the rice ball wrapped with the imitation crab.

MICKEY'S HAND PATTERN TOFU POUCH SUSHI

1 Stuff the tofu pouch with sushi rice, adjust its shape into a rectangle, and tie it with trefoil.

2 

Punch out Mickey's hand from the hanpen fish cake using a cutter and place it on **1**.

3 Glue the black sesame onto **2** using a small amount of mayonnaise.

INGREDIENTS

MICKEY THICK ROLL
(Amount for 1 roll)

- **Hanpen fish cake** (the rest of the hanpen will be used for the Mickey's hand pattern tofu pouch sushi) ···· 1 slice
- A
  - **Egg** ···· 1 egg
  - **Sugar** ···· ¼ teaspoon
  - **Powdered dashi** ···· small amount
  - **Potato starch or cornstarch** ···· small amount
- **Thick roll** ···· 1 roll

MICKEY LOGO SAUSAGE
(Amount for 1 sausage)

- **Tip of a frankfurter or sausage** ···· 1 piece
- **Cheese slice** ···· small amount

MICKEY MOUSE PANTS APPLE
(Amount for 1 piece)

- **Apple** ···· 1 slice

We used a cutter for this recipe, but you can also create a paper template to cut the hanpen fish cake pieces out.

MICKEY THICK ROLL

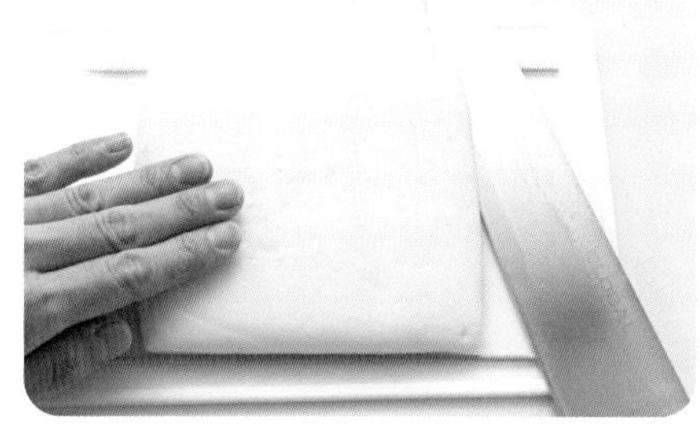

1 Place a bamboo skewer above and below the hanpen. Lay the kitchen knife sideways on the skewers and slice the hanpen into a thin sheet.

ATTENTION! You can create an evenly thin slice by cutting along the bamboo skewers.

2 Use a cutter to punch out the Mickey head silhouettes.

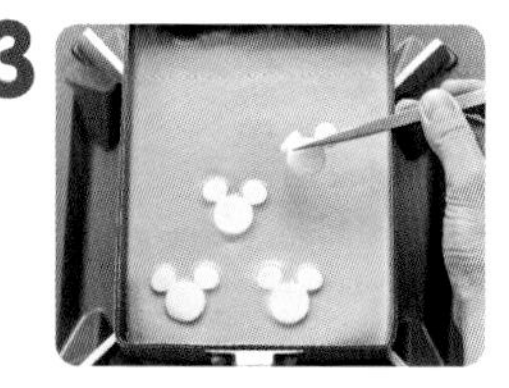

3 Mix the ingredients for **A**. Strain the mixture through a tea strainer and use cling wrap to remove the air bubbles (p. 9). Spread the egg mixture evenly in the frying pan. Turn off the heat once the egg mixture doesn't run down the pan when you tilt it (the surface should only be half-cooked but will keep its shape) and stick **2** onto it. If you're using cheese as a replacement, place Mickey cheese slices after the egg has cooled.

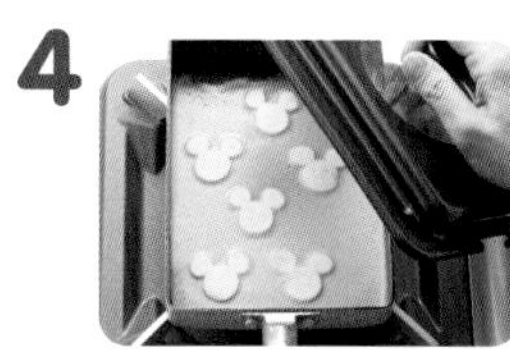

4 Turn the heat back on. Once the edge of the egg mixture has hardened, cover the lid and turn off the heat. Use the remaining heat to steam the egg.

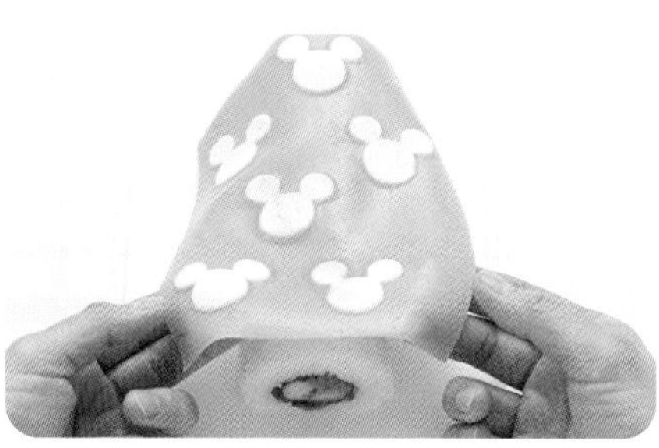

5 Use a knife to cut the edges of the egg to make a square, and then wrap the egg around the thick roll.

MICKEY LOGO SAUSAGE

1 Stick a thick straw into the frankfurter or sausage about 0.12 inch/3 mm deep.

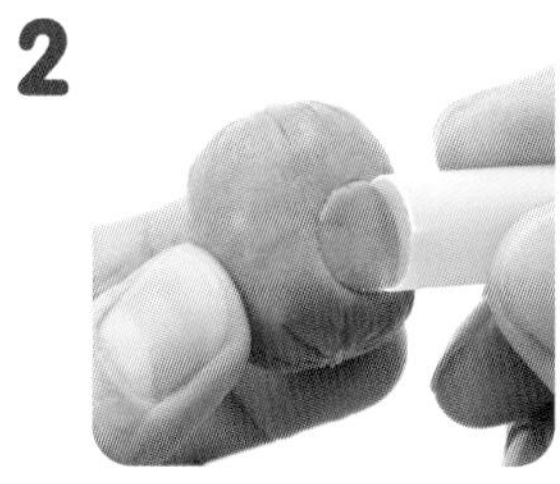

2 Tilt the straw diagonally and slide it across to the side to cut the surface of the sausage off.

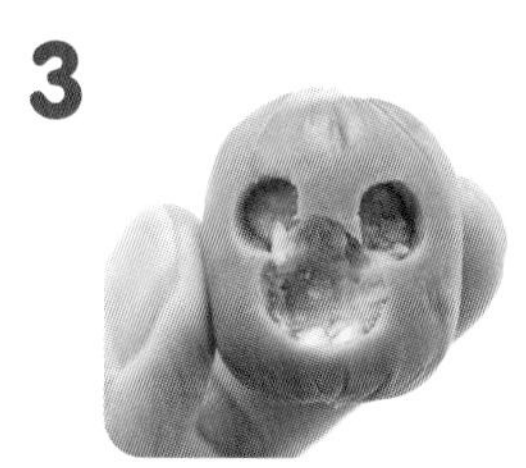

3 Use a thinner straw and cut out the ears with the same method as **1** and **2**.

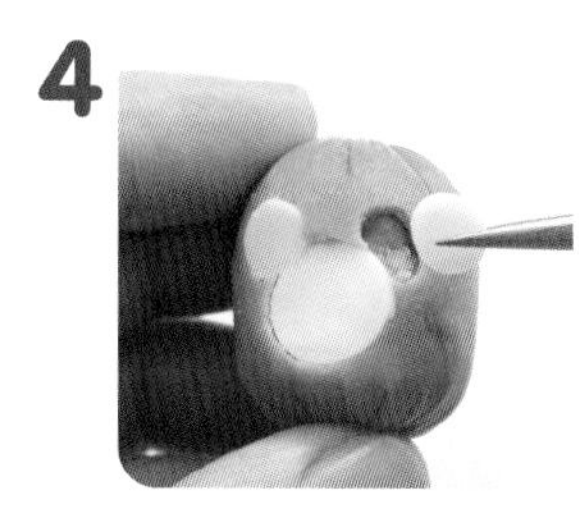

4 Punch out circles from the cheese slice with the straw you used to carve the holes and stuff cheese pieces into the holes you created in **3**.

MICKEY MOUSE PANTS APPLE

1 Cut the apple sideways in half and cut the edge off.

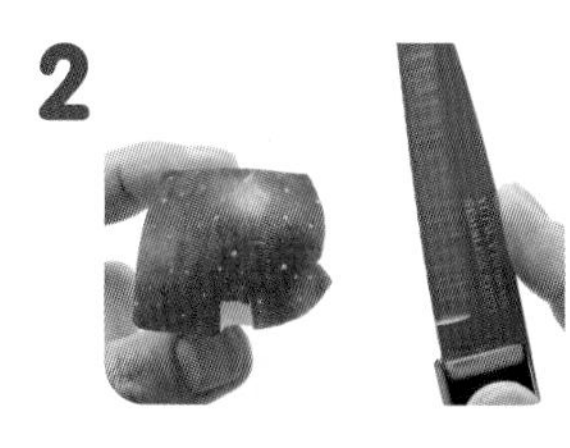

2 Use a knife to cut the apple piece into the shape of the pants.

3 Use a baller to carve out the buttons.

Mickey & Minnie's Birthday Cake

The handmade chocolate figures are so cute! Decorate them with heart-shaped strawberries.

INGREDIENTS

MICKEY & MINNIE CHOCOLATE FIGURES

Chocolate pen (black, red, white) .... as needed

STRAWBERRY HEART

Strawberry .... as needed

MINNIE MOTIF MARSHMALLOW FONDANT

Marshmallow (pink) .... 0.35 oz./10 g

Icing sugar .... 1 oz./30 g

Marshmallow (white) .... 0.35 oz./10 g

SPONGE CAKE

Cut in half to create two cakes. Place sliced strawberries on the base layer, cover with the top layer and frost with whipped cream.

RECIPE

MICKEY & MINNIE CHOCOLATE FIGURES

1

Fill a cup or bowl with warm water about 122°F/50°C. Leave the chocolate pen in the water and wait for the chocolate to soften.

2

Trace the illustration onto the baking paper.

3

Flip the baking paper over and trace the outline with the black chocolate pen.

ATTENTION! Use the back of the baking paper to trace the outline of the illustration.

4 Once the chocolate outline is set, fill the colored area with the chocolate pen.

5

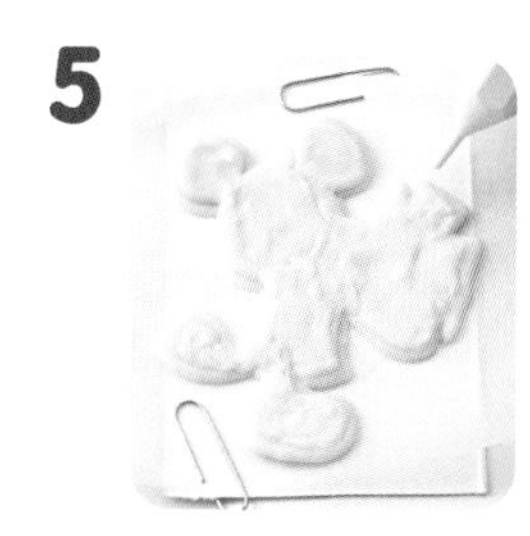

Once the colored area of the chocolate is set, cover the entire illustration with a layer of white chocolate about 0.2 inch/5 mm thick and refrigerate until hardened.

ATTENTION! The chocolate will crack easily if it's too thin, so make sure it's thick enough. Spread the white chocolate to make it slightly wider than the outline of the illustration.

6

Once **5** is hardened, peel off the baking paper and place Mickey on the decorated cake. Repeat steps **1–7** for Minnie.

STRAWBERRY HEART

Cut the strawberry in half lengthways and cut the strawberry cap off in a V shape.

MINNIE MOTIF MARSHMALLOW FONDANT (RIBBON)

1 Place the marshmallow (pink) inside a heat-resistant bowl and heat uncovered in the microwave for 20–30 seconds (the marshmallow should swell up and start to melt).

2 Add in 0.53 oz./15 g of sifted icing sugar into **1** and knead it until it's smooth (it will be hot right after being heated, so use a rubber spatula to mix it first and then use your hands to knead after it has cooled down).

3 Create the marshmallow (white) fondant dough by repeating steps **1** and **2**.

4

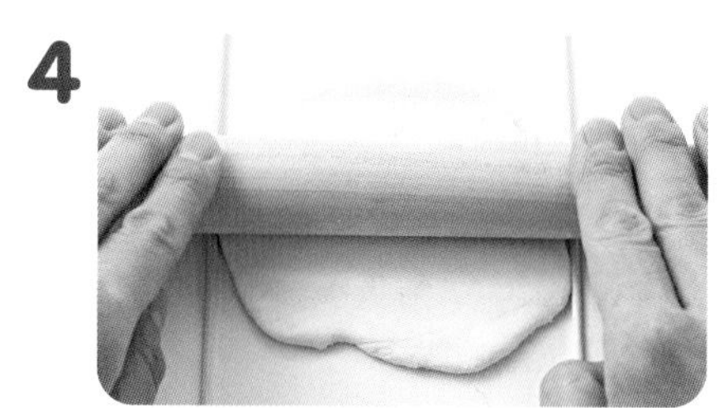

Sprinkle some icing sugar (not included in recipe amount) on the cutting board and roll the pink dough into a thin layer.

ATTENTION! Place a bamboo skewer on each side of the dough and use a rolling pin to evenly flatten the dough.

5

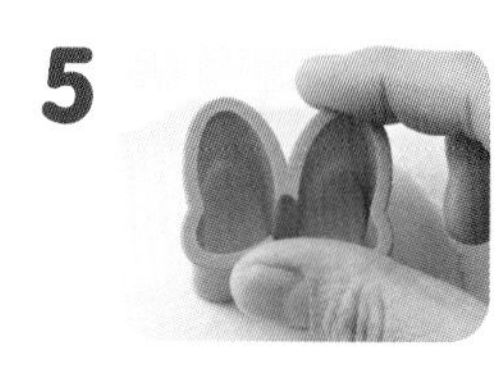

Use any cutter of your preference to punch out a shape.

6

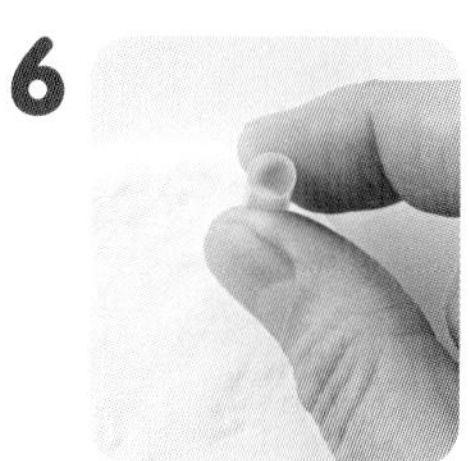

Roll the white dough flat and punch out circles with a straw. Place them on **5** to create the polka-dot patterns. (You can also create any pattern you like with your fingers and place that on the ribbons too.)

POOH

SPORTS DAY

Pooh & Piglet's Cheering Bento

This bento will give you the power to support your team!

BENTO MENU

- **Winnie the Pooh and friends rice balls** (Winnie the Pooh, Piglet, bees, numbers)
- **Quail egg Pooh**
- **Piglet fish sausage**
- **Honey jar**
- **Bee omelette**
- **Meatball** ▶p.89
- **Japanese omelette** ▶p.91
- **Asparagus bacon roll** ▶p.91
- **Ketchup pasta** ▶p.94
- **Carrot butterfly** (the feelers are made of deep-fried pasta), **cherry tomato, broccoli, lettuce**

INGREDIENTS

WINNIE THE POOH & FRIENDS RICE BALLS
(WINNIE THE POOH, PIGLET, BEES, NUMBERS)
(Amount for 9 rice balls)

- **Chicken or turkey breast** ········· 2 slices
- **Cheddar cheese** ········· 1 slice
- **Nori sheet** ········· As needed
- **Rice ball** (create your favorite rice ball and pack them into the bento box beforehand) ····· 9 rice balls
- **Deep-fried pasta** ···· as needed
- **Dark-pink soft salami** ··· 1 slice
- **Cheese slice** ········· ½ slice
- **Thinly sliced carrots** (0.2 inch/5 mm slices, boiled in salted water) ···· 3 slices

RECIPE

WINNIE THE POOH & FRIENDS RICE BALLS

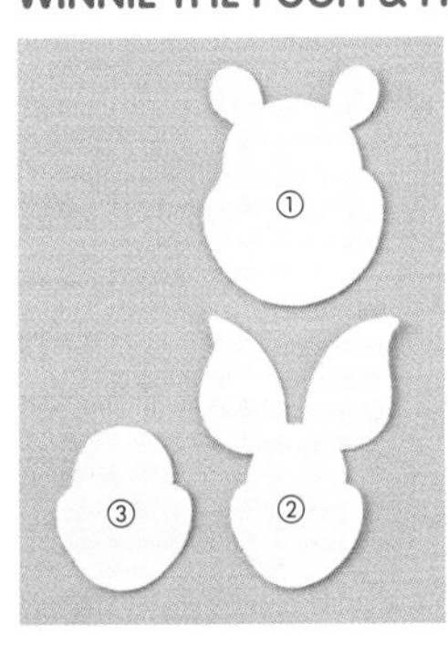

Create the paper pattern templates out of a milk carton (① Pooh's Outline, ② Piglet's Outline, ③ Piglet's Face).

POOH

1 Place paper template ① on the ham and cheddar cheese. Cut around it and place the cheddar cheese outline on top of the ham outline.

2 Cut the nori sheet to create the eyes, nose, mouth, eyebrows, lines of the nose, and the lines of the chin, and glue them onto **1**.

3 Create one more Pooh and attach the faces to the rice balls with deep-fried pasta.

PIGLET

1 Place paper template ② on the salami and cut around it.

2 Place paper template ③ on the ham. Cut around it and place it on **1**.

3 Squeeze a straw into a triangle shape, punch the nose out of the salami, and place it on **2**.

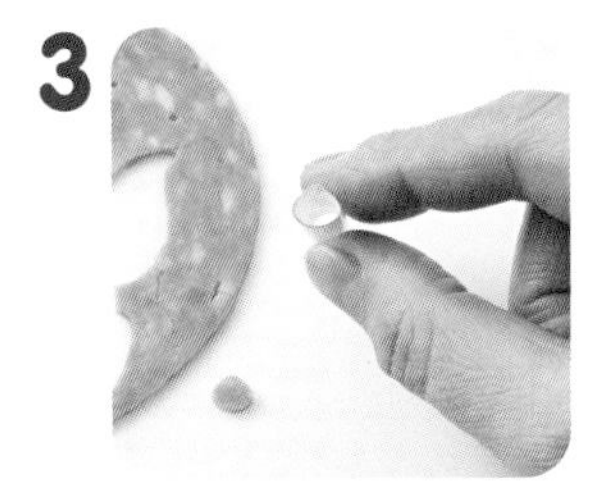

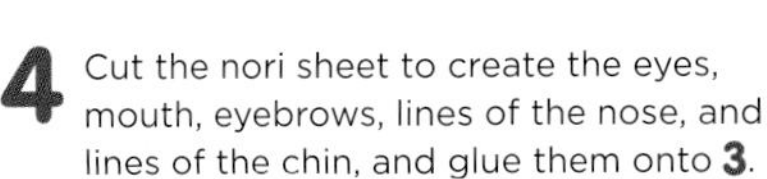

4 Cut the nori sheet to create the eyes, mouth, eyebrows, lines of the nose, and lines of the chin, and glue them onto **3**.

5 Create one more Piglet and attach the faces to the rice balls with deep-fried pasta.

BEE

1 Use an oval cutter to punch an oval shape out from a cheddar cheese slice, and glue it onto the ham.

2 Use the top half of the oval cutter that you used in **1** to cut out half an oval from the cheese slice. After removing the half oval, use the top half of a heart-shaped cutter to punch out the wings as shown in the picture. Place the wings on the ham with **1**.

3 Trim the excess ham around it.

4 Cut the pattern of the body, eyes, and mouth out of the nori sheet and glue them onto **3**.

5 Create one more bee and attach both bees to the rice balls with deep-fried pasta.

INGREDIENTS

QUAIL EGG WINNIE THE POOH (Amount for 1 egg)

- **Quail egg** ······ 1 egg
- **Curry liquid mixture:**
  - Water ······ 50 ml
  - Curry powder ······ ¼ teaspoon
  - Salt ······ a dash
- **Corn** ······ 2 kernels
- **Deep-fried pasta** ······ as needed

PIGLET FISH SAUSAGE

- **Fish sausage** (0.2 inch/5 mm slice) ······ 1 slice
- **Dark-pink soft salami** ······ small amount

HONEY JAR

- **Ham** ······ ½ slice
- **Cheddar cheese** ······ ¼ slice
- **Nori sheet** ······ as needed

BEE OMELETTE

- **Japanese omelette** (0.4 inch/1 cm thick) ······ 1 omelette
- **Thinly sliced kamaboko fish cake** ······ 1 slice
- **Nori sheet** ······ as needed

Paper Pattern Template Examples

The shape of Piglet's ears and his facial expression have been changed to make it easier to create the bento.

NUMBER

Use a flower-shaped cutter to cut the carrot and use a number cutter to punch out the number from the center of the carrot. Create numbers 1–3 and attach them onto the rice balls with deep-fried pasta.

QUAIL EGG WINNIE THE POOH

1

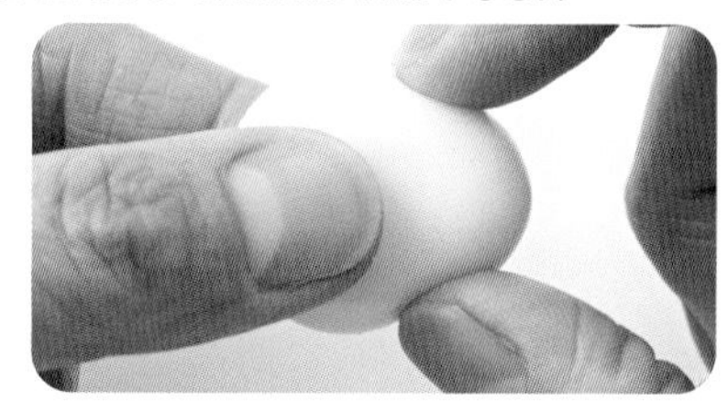

Boil the quail egg in hot water for about 8 minutes, remove the eggshell, and gently mold the egg into the shape of Pooh's face while it is still hot. Marinate the egg in the curry liquid mixture for 15–30 minutes.

2

Attach the corn kernels onto the top of **1** with deep-fried pasta.

PIGLET FISH SAUSAGE

1

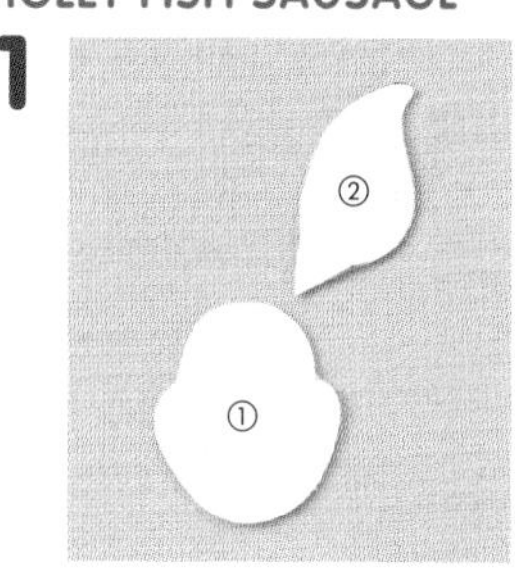

Create the paper pattern templates out of a milk carton (① Piglet's Face, ② Piglet's Ear).

2

Place paper template ① on a slice of the fish sausage and cut around it.

3

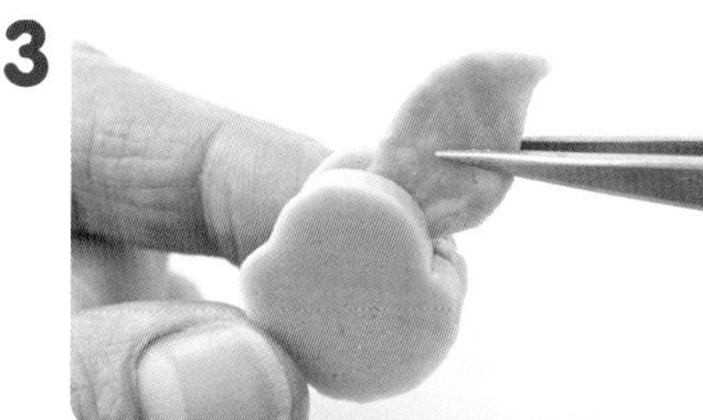

Place paper template ② on the soft salami and cut two ears out (flip one over to use as the opposite ear). Score the top of **2** and insert the ears into it.

HONEY JAR

1

Create a paper template for the honey jar out of a milk carton.

2 Place the honey jar paper template on the ham and cheddar cheese and cut around it. Place the cheddar cheese piece on top of the ham.

3

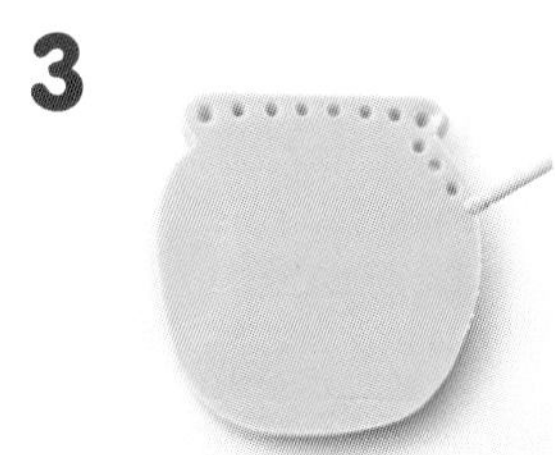

Use a toothpick to create the dot pattern around the edge of the cheddar cheese.

4 Cut the "POOH" letters out of the nori sheet and glue them onto **3**.

BEE OMELETTE

1 Make a shallow cut in the middle of the Japanese omelette. Use a heart-shaped cutter to punch out the wings from the fish cake and insert them into the gap.

2 Cut the patterns of the body and eyes out of the nori sheet and glue them onto **1**.

Mickey & Minnie's Pumpkin Pudding

Mickey and Minnie have turned into pumpkins!

INGREDIENTS

Chocolate pen (orange, black) ····· as needed (fill a cup or bowl with warm water about 122°F/50°C and leave the chocolate pen in the water until the chocolate melts)
Pumpkin-shaped marshmallow ····· 2 pieces
Pumpkin seed ··················· ½ (cut lengthwise)
Ready-made pumpkin puddings ·· 2 puddings
Whipped cream ·························· as needed

Paper Pattern Template Example

RECIPE

MICKEY & MINNIE MARSHMALLOWS

1

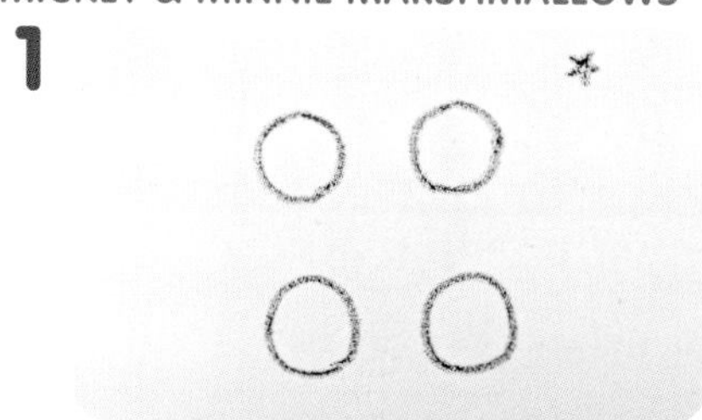

Draw Mickey and Minnie's ears (four circles) on the baking paper.

2

Flip **1** over and use the orange chocolate pen to fill in the circle at a thickness of about 0.12 inch/3 mm. Refrigerate until the chocolate is completely set.

3

Squeeze some chocolate from the chocolate pen into a small bowl. Dip the tip of a toothpick into the chocolate and draw Mickey's face on the marshmallows.

ATTENTION! It will be easier to draw delicate patterns with a toothpick rather than with the chocolate pen. Using a silicon bowl for the melted chocolate will make cleaning much easier. The chocolate will be easy to remove once it has set.

4

Using the same method as in **3**, draw Minnie's face on the other marshmallow.

5

Use a pair of scissors to create an incision for each of the ears. Do the same on Mickey's marshmallow.

6

Place the ears from **2** into the incisions created in **5**.

7 Stick the pumpkin seed into the top of marshmallow Mickey's head. Stick a ribbon-shaped pick into the top of marshmallow Minnie's head.

CHOCOLATE BAT AND MOON

1

Trace the illustration of the bat and moon onto the baking paper.

2

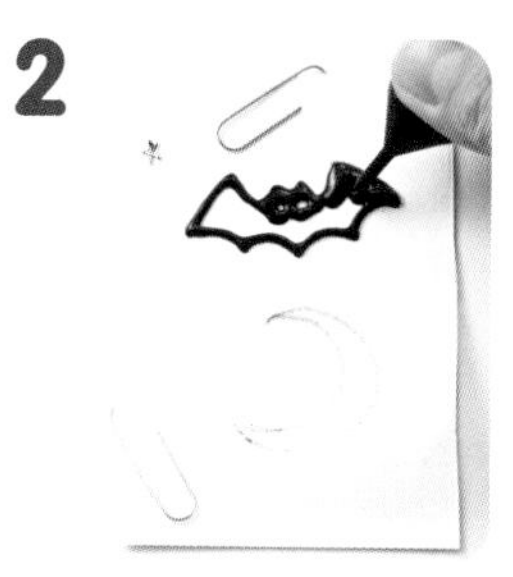

Flip **1** over, use the black chocolate pen to fill in the illustration at a thickness of about 0.12 inch/3 mm, and set the chocolate inside the fridge.

3

Pipe some whipped cream onto the surface of each of the pumpkin puddings. Peel off the bat and the moon from the baking paper. Flip them over and place one on each of the dollops of whipped cream. Then place the Mickey or Minnie marshmallow in each of the puddings.

CHRISTMAS

Mickey's Christmas Platter

He can't wait for Christmas!

BENTO MENU

- Ketchup chicken rice Mickey
- Santa's boot, Santa's hat sausage
- Mickey meatloaf
- Christmas tree canapé
- Corn salad in a cherry tomato cup
- Lotus root chip snow crystal
- Soup with Mickey's hand croutons
- Mickey's no-bake cheesecake
- Sweet potato star (simmered in lemon juice), baby leaves

INGREDIENTS

KETCHUP CHICKEN RICE MICKEY

- **Ketchup chicken rice** ··· as needed
- **Scrambled egg** ··· as needed
- **Glazed carrot** (0.2 inch/5 mm slices) ··· 2 slices
- **Pasta** ··· as needed

SANTA'S BOOT, SANTA'S HAT

- **Bite-size cheese** ··· 1 piece
- **Little smokie** (about 2.4 inches/6 cm long) ··· 1 sausage
- **Deep-fried pasta** ··· as needed
- **Cheddar cheese** ··· small amount

MICKEY MEATLOAF

- **Onion** ··· ¼ onion
- **Panko or other bread crumbs** ··· 2 tablespoons
- **Milk** ··· 2 tablespoons
- **Ground pork or beef** ··· ⅓ lbs.
- **Mixed vegetables** ··· 1 oz./30 g
- **Beaten egg** ··· ½ egg
- **Salt** ··· roughly ¼ tablespoon
- **Pepper, nutmeg** ··· to season
- **Quail eggs** (boiled) ··· 4 eggs
- **Baby corn** ··· 4 pieces
- **Pasta** ··· as needed
- **Bacon** ··· 3 slices

RECIPE

KETCHUP CHICKEN RICE MICKEY

1

Place cling wrap in a rice bowl, fill the bowl with ketchup chicken rice, and adjust its shape.

2

Place **1** on the plate and surround the rice with scrambled egg.

3

Create two incisions on the top of the chicken rice head and attach the carrot ears with deep-fried pasta.

4

Attach the Santa hat* on top of the head with deep-fried pasta.

*Recipe on right.

SANTA'S BOOT, SANTA'S HAT SAUSAGE

Cut the bite-size cheese into three slices. Cut the little smokie into two pieces at around 0.8 inch/2 cm length to create a ⅔ piece **(a)** and a ⅓ piece **(b)**.

SANTA'S BOOT

1

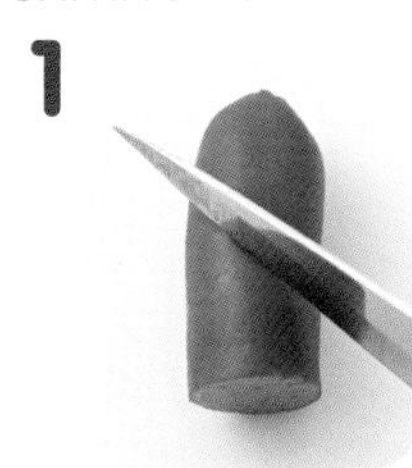

Place the little smokie piece **(a)** lengthwise on the cutting board and cut it diagonally into two pieces. Flip one of the pieces over and connect the cut ends together.

2

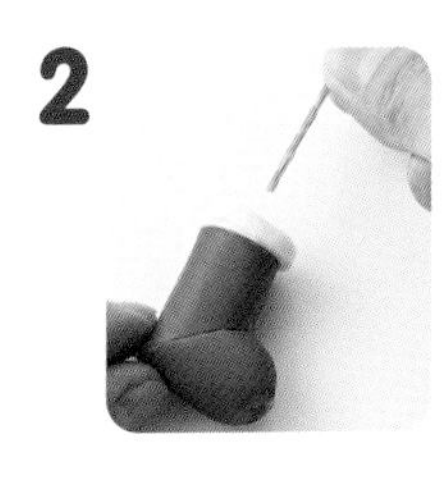

Place the slice of bite-size cheese on top of **1** and thread the entire boot together with a long piece of deep-fried pasta.

3 Use a star-shaped cutter to punch out a star from the cheddar cheese and place it on **2**.

SANTA'S HAT

1 Connect the end of little smokie piece **(b)** to one of the bite-size cheese pieces.

2 Use a round piping tip to punch out the pom-pom from the remaining slice of bite-size cheese.

3 Use a long piece of deep-fried pasta to attach **1** and **2** together.

MICKEY MEATLOAF

1 Mince the onions, add a small amount of butter, and heat in the microwave for about 1–2 minutes. Let the minced onion cool. Soak the panko or bread crumbs in milk.

2 Add **1** and the mixed vegetables, beaten egg, salt, pepper, and nutmeg into the ground meat and mix thoroughly.

3

Get out a large sheet of baking paper. Spread ⅓ of **2** onto the baking paper and line it up lengthways with the quail eggs. Place the baby corn on both sides of the quail egg and use the pasta to lock them in place.

Note: We do not recommend substituting cheese for quail eggs in this recipe, as it will melt.

4 Fill the gap in between the baby corn with **2**. Evenly spread out the rest of **2** to cover the entire meatloaf. Lift up both edges of the baking sheet to adjust its shape.

5

Wrap the meatloaf with bacon.

6

Wrap the meatloaf and the baking sheet with aluminum foil and bake in a toaster oven for about 20 minutes. Open the top of the wrapping (aluminum foil and baking paper) and bake for another 8–10 minutes to brown the surface of the meatloaf. Let the meatloaf cool and then cut it into slices.

INGREDIENTS

CHRISTMAS TREE CANAPÉ
(Amount for 4 trees)

- **Potato** ········· 1 small potato
- **Broccoli crown** (boiled in salted water) ········· 5–6 florets
- **Mayonnaise** ········· 1 tablespoon
- **Sugar, salt, pepper** ········· small amount of each
- **Milk** ········· 1–2 tablespoons
- **Crackers** ········· 4 pieces
- **Bell pepper** (red, yellow; boiled in salted water) ········· small amount of each

CORN SALAD IN A CHERRY TOMATO CUP
(Amount for 1 cup)

- **Large cherry tomato** (or medium tomato) ········· 1 tomato
- **Corn** ········· as needed

LOTUS ROOT CHIP SNOW CRYSTALS
(Amount for 3 slices)

- **Lotus root** ········· 3 slices
- **Frying oil** ········· as needed
- **Salt** ········· as needed

SOUP WITH MICKEY'S HAND CROUTONS
(Amount for 9 Mickey hands)

- **Sandwich bread** ········· 1 slice
- **Favorite soup** ········· as needed

MICKEY'S NO-BAKE CHEESECAKE
(Amount for 1 cake)

- **No-bake cheesecake** ········· 1 cake
- **Cocoa powder** (sweetened) ········· as needed
- **Green tea powder** (sweetened) ········· as needed

RECIPE

CHRISTMAS TREE CANAPÉ

1 Mash the boiled potato and then mix it with the chopped broccoli, mayonnaise, sugar, salt, and pepper. Slowly stir in a small amount of milk a little bit at a time until the mixture is smooth and even.

2

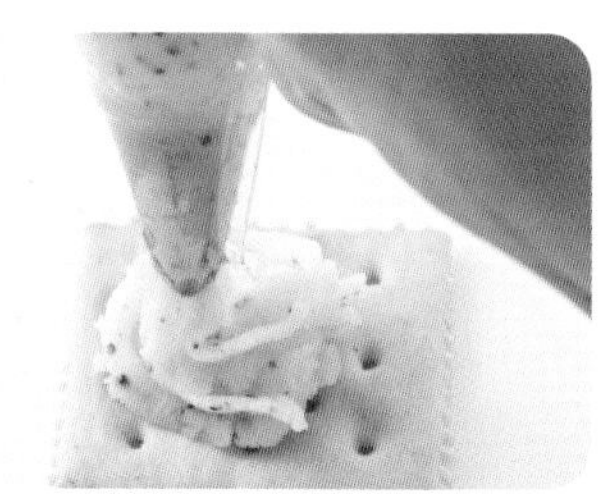

Put the mashed potato in a piping bag with a star piping tip and pipe onto the cracker. Place a star-shaped pick on top of the mashed potato.

3

Punch out Mickey's head and ears with large and small piping tips on the red and yellow bell peppers.

4

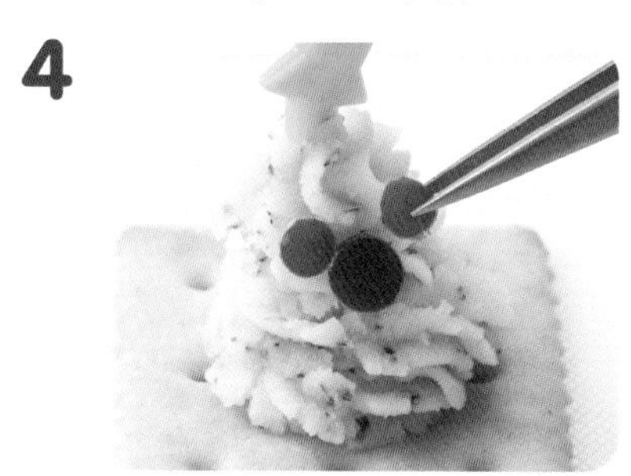

Stick **3** on **2** as Mickey ornaments.

CORN SALAD IN A CHERRY TOMATO CUP

1 Cut off the top ¼ of the cherry tomato.

2

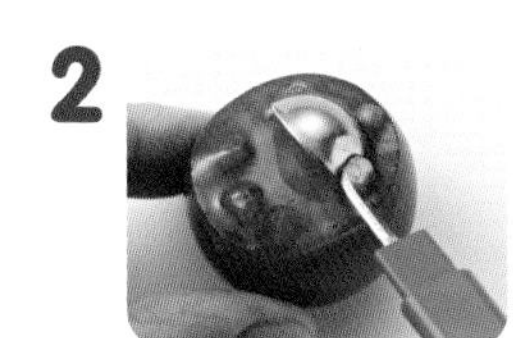

Scoop out the insides of the cherry tomato with a melon baller. Stuff the tomato with corn and place **1** next to it.

LOTUS ROOT CHIP SNOW CRYSTALS

1 Peel off the skin of the lotus root and slice it into 0.04 inch/1 mm slices. Soak the slices in water in a small bowl. Add 1 teaspoon of white vinegar into the water. Make sure that the lotus root pieces are completely submerged.

2

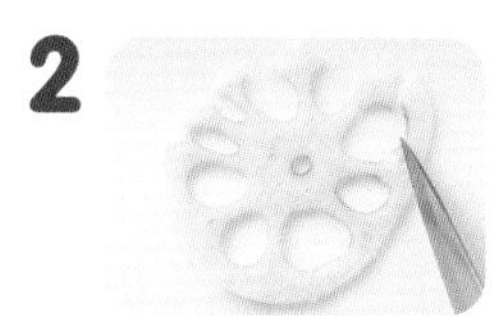

Dry **1** and cut off the edges of the lotus root in a V shape so that they look like snowflakes with many arrows.

3 Deep-fry **2** in 338°F/170°C oil until the lotus root pieces turn brown. Sprinkle salt on the snowflakes before serving.

SOUP WITH MICKEY'S HAND CROUTONS

1

Use a Mickey hand cutter to punch the hands out of the sandwich bread (alternatively, you can use the paper pattern template example on p. 75 and cut the hands out with a pair of scissors).

2 Place **1** in a heat-resistant dish and microwave it for 1 minute. Do not overlap the bread pieces or cover them with anything.

3 Flip the bread hands from **2** and microwave them for another minute. Keep your eye on the bread and adjust the microwave time to make sure the bread is crispy.

4 Pour your favorite soup in a cup. Sprinkle dried parsley over it and place **3** gently on the surface.

MICKEY'S NO-BAKE CHEESECAKE

1

Create the paper pattern template out of a milk carton.

2

Place **1** on top of the no-bake cheesecake and sift cocoa powder on top of it.

3

Remove the paper template from **2** and use a spoon to sprinkle green tea powder around the edge of the cake. Insert a holly pick into the cake.

EAT UP! SIDE DISHES

The amount of oil used to cook the food, the amount of salt and pepper, and the amount of flour are all "as needed" if not specified.

Unless stated otherwise, the recipe is for 1 serving. You will need to adjust the amount you cook depending on the size of the bento box.

Meat

CHICKEN

Deep-Fried Chicken Tenders with Almonds

① Crush ¼ cup of sliced almonds into coarse pieces.

② Remove the tendon from a chicken tender, cut the meat open, season it with salt and pepper, and wrap 3 frozen string beans in it.

③ Coat ② with a layer of flour, a layer of beaten egg, and a layer of ①. Deep-fry the chicken tender in 356°F/180°C oil until it turns golden brown.

Mayo-Teriyaki Chicken

① Mix 2 teaspoons of soy sauce, 2 teaspoons of sake, 2 teaspoons of mirin, 1 tablespoon of sugar, and ½ tablespoon of mayonnaise.

② Cut 2.1 oz./60 g of chicken thigh in half and season it with a small amount of sake and potato starch (or cornstarch). Pan-fry with sesame oil until it turns brown. Use a paper towel to remove any excess oil in the pan, and then add ① and cook until the sauce thickens.

Chicken and Sweet Potato Stir-Fry

① Chop ¼ of a sweet potato into large chunks and heat the pieces in a microwave for about 1 minute.

② Cut 2.1 oz./60 g of chicken thigh into bite-size pieces. Season it with salt and pepper and coat it with a thin layer of potato starch (or cornstarch).

③ Heat some vegetable oil and pan-fry ②. Once the chicken is cooked, add in sweet potatoes, 1 ½ teaspoons of soy sauce and sugar, and 1 teaspoon of vinegar. Cook until the sauce is thickened.

Colorful Sweet and Sour Chicken

① Mix 2 teaspoons of soy sauce, 2 teaspoons of vinegar, 2 teaspoons of sugar, 1 teaspoon of ketchup and 1 teaspoon of sake.

② Cut Japanese fried chicken into bite-size pieces. Use a star-shaped cutter to punch the stars out from the red, green, and yellow bell peppers. Cut the onion into wedges. If you are in a hurry, you can use precooked chicken nuggets as a substitute for the fried chicken.

③ Heat vegetable oil in a frying pan, stir-fry ②, add ①, and stir-fry even more.

Japanese Fried Chicken on a Pick/ Japanese Fried Chicken

(Easy-to-cook amount)

① Cut 2 chicken thighs into bite-size pieces.

② Place ① inside a plastic bag, add in 1 inch of ginger (ground), 1 clove garlic (ground), ½ tablespoon of sake and soy sauce, and a small amount of salt and pepper. Massage the plastic bag and marinate the chicken for at least 20 minutes.

③ Coat ② with 6 tablespoons of flour and fry it in 356°F/180°C oil until it turns golden brown.

PORK

Bell Pepper Meat Roll

① Cut approximately ⅛ of a red, yellow, and orange bell pepper into strips.

② Season 2 slices of thinly sliced pork with salt and pepper. Wrap ① with the pork.

③ Heat vegetable oil in a frying pan. Coat ② in flour and cook it until it turns brown. Add 1 teaspoon of soy sauce, 1 teaspoon of mirin, 1 teaspoon of sake, and ½ teaspoon of sugar and dress the meat roll with the sauce.

Flower Pattern Meat Roll

① Boil 1 baby corn and 2 snap peas.

② Season 2 thin pork slices with salt and pepper and wrap ① with the meat.

③ Heat the frying pan with vegetable oil, lightly coat ② in flour, and grill until brown. Add 1 teaspoon of soy sauce, 1 teaspoon of mirin, 1 teaspoon of sake, and ½ teaspoon of sugar and dress the meat roll with the sauce.

Carrot and Bean Meat Roll

① Boil 2 slices of carrot (0.4 inch/1 cm size sticks with a crisscross cut in them) and 2 string beans in salted water.

② Season 2 thin slices of pork with salt and pepper. Wrap ① with the pork.

③ Heat vegetable oil in a frying pan. Coat ② in flour and cook it until it turns brown. Mix 1 teaspoon of soy sauce and 1 teaspoon of sake with ½ teaspoon of sugar for the sauce, and dress the meat with the sauce.

Broccoli Meatball (Enough to make 2)

① Add 1 tablespoon of minced onion, 1 tablespoon of beaten egg, ¼ teaspoon of powdered chicken stock, ¼ teaspoon of sugar, and a little salt to 2.1 oz./60 g of ground pork, and mix thoroughly.

② Coat two florets of broccoli with flour and wrap in ①.

③ Fry ② in 356°F/180°C oil until it turns golden brown.

GROUND MEAT

Japanese Meatloaf (Easy-to-cook amount)

① Thoroughly mix ½ tablespoon of panko or bread crumbs, ½ teaspoon of miso, 1 teaspoon of sake, and a small amount of ground ginger with 1.8 oz./50 g of ground chicken. Spread the ground meat out on a piece of cling wrap.

② Cut an asparagus stalk into 3 pieces and place on ①. Wrap it up and heat the roll in a microwave for about 90 seconds.

③ Remove the cling wrap and wrap the meat with ⅔ slice of thin omelette sheet.

Carrot and Pork Patty

① Thoroughly mix 1 tablespoon of minced onion, 1 tablespoon of panko, 1 tablespoon of ground carrot, and a dash of salt, pepper, and nutmeg with 2.1 oz./60 g of ground pork.

② Split ① into 2 portions and shape them. Heat the vegetable oil and pan-fry patties until they turn brown.

③ Add 2 teaspoons of ketchup, 1 teaspoon of Worcestershire sauce, and a small amount of honey to the pan and coat the patties with the sauce.

Colorful Patty

① Thoroughly mix 1 tablespoon of minced onion, 1 tablespoon of panko, 1 tablespoon of ground carrot, and a dash of salt, pepper, and nutmeg with 2.1 oz./60 g of ground pork.

② Shape the patties. Heat the vegetable oil and pan-fry the patties until they turn brown.

③ Add 1 teaspoon of soy sauce, 1 teaspoon of mirin, 1 teaspoon of sake, and ½ teaspoon of sugar to the pan and coat the patties with the sauce.

Stuffed Bell Pepper

① Thoroughly mix 1 tablespoon of minced onion, 1 tablespoon of beaten egg, ¼ teaspoon of powdered chicken stock, ¼ teaspoon of sugar, and a little salt with 2.1 oz./60 g of ground pork.

② Cut 2 0.4 inch/1 cm slices of green bell pepper and stuff ① into them.

③ Heat the vegetable oil and pan-fry ② until the bell peppers turn brown.

Meatball (Easy-to-cook amount)

① Thoroughly mix ½ of a beaten egg, ¼ teaspoon of salt, 1 teaspoon of sugar, ½ small onion (minced), ½ tablespoon of potato starch or cornstarch with 7 oz./200 g of ground pork until the mixture turns sticky.

② Roll ① into bite-size balls and deep-fry them in 356°F/180°C oil until they turn golden brown.

HAM AND SAUSAGES

Ham and Cheese Roll

① Leave the cheese slice out for 3-5 minutes until it gets soft. Place it on a piece of soft salami and roll the 2 slices together.

② Once the roll in ① is set, cut it into bite-size pieces.

Sautéed Sausage and Mushrooms

① Cut the sausages into bite-size slices. Cut off the bottom stem of 5-6 shimeji mushrooms and separate them into small bunches. You can find shimeji mushrooms in Japanese and Asian supermarkets, or you can substitute any other type of mushroom.

② Melt some butter in a heated frying pan. Sauté ① and season it with a dash of soy sauce, salt, and pepper.

Sautéed Sausage with Bell Peppers

① Cut the sausage into diagonal slices. Cut ⅛ of the red bell pepper and ⅛ of the yellow bell pepper into chunks. Cut off the bottom stem of 5-6 shimeji mushrooms and separate them into small bunches.

② Heat vegetable oil in a frying pan, sauté ①, and season with a pinch of herb salt.

Sausage and Bell Pepper Stir-Fry

① Score the surface of 3 little smokies. Cut ⅛ of red, yellow, and orange bell peppers into chunks.

② Heat vegetable oil in a frying pan and stir-fry ①. Add 1 teaspoon of ketchup and a pinch of salt and pepper and continue to stir-fry until the sauce thickens.

Seafood/ Processed Food

SALMON

Grilled Salmon Wrapped in Nori

① Mix together ½ tablespoon of soy sauce, ½ tablespoon of sake, and a pinch of ground ginger juice.

② Cut ½ slice of salmon into bite-size portions and marinate them in ① for about 15 minutes.

③ Wrap ② with strips of nori. Place them on a baking tray lined with aluminum foil and roast them in a toaster oven for about 8 minutes.

Salmon Stir-Fried in Sweet Vinegar

① Mix together 1 ½ teaspoons of vinegar, 1 ½ teaspoons of sugar, and 1 teaspoon of soy sauce.

② Cut ½ slice of salmon into bite-size portions and coat them with a layer of potato starch (or cornstarch).

③ Heat some ground ginger in a frying pan with vegetable oil until the ginger becomes fragrant. Pan-fry ② and pour ① evenly into the pan. Garnish the dish with some turnip greens that have been boiled in salted water on the side.

Salmon Roll

① Remove the bones and skin from ½ slice of salmon and mince the salmon finely with a kitchen knife.

② Thoroughly mix 1 tablespoon of minced onion, 1 tablespoon of panko (or bread crumbs), 1 teaspoon of mayonnaise, and a dash of salt, pepper, and squeezed ground ginger juice with the salmon. Spread the salmon on a square-cut nori sheet and roll it from the side.

③ Deep-fry in 356°F/180°C oil for 2–3 minutes and wrap it with ⅔ slice of omelette sheet.

Salmon Patty

① Remove the bones and skin from ½ slice of salmon and mince it finely with a kitchen knife.

② Thoroughly mix 1 tablespoon of minced onion, 1 tablespoon of panko (or bread crumbs), 1 teaspoon of mayonnaise, and a dash of salt, pepper, and squeezed ground ginger juice with the salmon. Split the salmon into two portions and shape them into patties.

③ Press a couple of shimeji mushrooms that have been lightly coated with flour into the salmon patties. Pan-fry them with vegetable oil until both patties are browned.

PRAWN

Mayonnaise Prawn

① Mix 2 teaspoons of mayonnaise, ½ teaspoon of ketchup, and a dash of powdered chicken stock together.

② Devein 3 prawns and boil them in salted water for about 2 minutes.

③ Coat ② in ① and sprinkle some chopped snow pea (boiled in salted water) over it.

Prawn and Broccoli Mayo Salad

① Mix together 2 teaspoons of mayonnaise, ½ teaspoon of ketchup, and a small amount of powdered chicken stock.

② Boil a small amount of broccoli in salted water. Devein 3 prawns and boil in salted water for about 2 minutes.

③ Dress ② with ①.

Scrambled Egg with Prawn and Asparagus

① Boil asparagus and 3 prawns in salted water for about 30 seconds and cut asparagus into diagonal slices.

② Mix together 1 egg, 2 teaspoons of milk, a pinch of powdered beef stock, and a small amount of mayonnaise.

③ Heat olive oil in a frying pan and stir-fry ①. Add ② and rapidly stir with a pair of cooking chopsticks until the egg is cooked.

SWORDFISH

Swordfish Sautéed with Ketchup

① Cut the ½ slice swordfish into bite-size pieces. Season with salt and pepper and let it rest for 5–10 minutes. Then wipe off any excess moisture and coat the fish with a thin layer of flour.

② Heat the vegetable oil and pan-fry ① until it turns brown. Add ½ tablespoon of ketchup, ½ tablespoon of Worcestershire sauce, ½ teaspoon of soy sauce, and a small amount of honey. Cook until the sauce thickens.

COD

Cod Wrapped in Bacon

① Cut the bacon slice in half.

② Cut the ½ slice of cod into bite-size pieces and season with a small amount of salt and sake. Let the fish rest for 5–10 minutes and wipe off any excess moisture.

③ Wrap ① around ② and pan-fry it with olive oil. Fry the side with the wrapped end first.

IMITATION CRAB

Broccoli and Imitation Crab Dressed in Mayonnaise

① Boil 2 florets of broccoli in salted water.

② Cut the imitation crab into 0.4 inch/1 cm pieces.

③ Dress ① and ② with 1 teaspoon of mayonnaise and a small amount of Japanese noodle soup base.

Lotus Root and Imitation Crab Salad

① Cut 1.2 inches/3 cm of lotus root into thin slices and boil them in hot water with a small amount of vinegar. Boil one or two string beans in salted water and cut diagonally. Cut the imitation crab into 0.4 inch/1 cm pieces.

② Put ① in a bowl and mix together with 1 teaspoon of mayonnaise and a small amount of dashi soy sauce.*

*Dashi shoyu, or dashi soy sauce, is a mixture of soy sauce and Japanese soup broth. If you can't find it premade in the store, you can mix dashi with soy sauce or just use soy sauce on its own.

CHIKUWA FISH CAKE

Chikuwa Fish Cake Flower

① Cut ½ stick of chikuwa in two and cut a cross into the cut end of each piece.

② Cut ½ slice of ham in two, fold and roll the ham piece sideways, and stick into the chikuwa from ①.

③ Create another chikuwa flower using the remaining ingredients.

Simmered Chikuwa Fish Cake and Vegetables

① Cut the chikuwa into diagonal slices.

② Pour 100 ml of water and 1 tablespoon of kelp dashi broth (triple-concentrated type) into a pot. Add ①, 2 slices of half-circle carrots, and 2–3 shimeji mushrooms, and boil for about 5 minutes. Add some diagonally cut string beans and let the flavor seep into the ingredients.

Egg

Japanese Omelette (Easy-to-cook amount)

① Mix 1 egg, ½ teaspoon of kelp dashi broth (triple-concentrated type), 1 tablespoon of water, and 1 teaspoon of sugar together.

② Heat a small amount of vegetable oil in a Japanese omelette pan, pour in about ⅓ of the egg mixture, and roll the egg toward you from the far end.

③ Once you've finished rolling, push the egg back to the far end, pour in a little more egg mixture, and repeat this procedure until you use up all the egg mixture.

Mitsuba and Shirasu Omelette

Mitsuba and shirasu can be found in some Japanese supermarkets. Mitsuba is a kind of Japanese herb used in cooking and garnishing. The shirasu, or semi-dried whitebait, used in this recipe is labeled as "shirasu boshi" in Japanese supermarkets.

If you can't find these ingredients, you can use the same amount of parsley or coriander to replace the mitsuba and leave out the shirasu.

① Cut ¼ of the mitsuba bundle into 0.4 inch/1 cm lengths.

② Mix ①, 1 egg, 1 teaspoon of concentrated dashi broth, 1 tablespoon of water, and 1 teaspoon of semi-dried whitebait together.

③ Heat a small amount of vegetable oil in a Japanese omelette pan. Pour in about ⅓ of the egg mixture and roll the egg toward you from the far end. Once you've finished rolling, push the egg back to the far end, and pour in a little more egg mixture. Repeat this procedure until you use up all the egg mixture.

Vegetables

ASPARAGUS

Asparagus Sautéed with Herbs

① Slice 2 stalks of asparagus diagonally and sauté them in a heated frying pan with olive oil.

② Once the asparagus is cooked, season it with a small amount of herb salt.

Asparagus Bacon Roll

① Cut a slice of bacon in half.

② Cut two stalks of asparagus diagonally in 1.2 inch/3 cm sections and boil them in salted water for about 30 seconds.

③ Wrap the bacon around ② and pan-fry it with vegetable oil until it is slightly browned.

TURNIP

Sautéed Turnip with Herbs

① Cut ½ a turnip into wedges and pan-fry it with olive oil.

② Once the turnip is cooked, season it with a small amount of herb salt.

PUMPKIN

Pumpkin Dressed with Powdered Cheese

① Slowly pan-fry 3 slices of pumpkin (0.2 inch/5 mm slices) with vegetable oil.

② Sprinkle and coat ① with ½ teaspoon of powdered cheese.

Simmered Pumpkin

① Mix 1 tablespoon of milk, ½ teaspoon of sugar, and a small amount of salt in a bowl.

② Heat a slice of frozen pumpkin in a microwave for about 1 minute. Cut into two pieces while it's still hot and marinate the pumpkin in ①.

③ Add a couple of raisins to ②, flip the pumpkin over after 10–15 minutes, and keep marinating it until it cools down.

Pumpkin and Sweet Potato Salad (Easy-to-cook amount)

① Cut ¼ of the pumpkin and sweet potato into bite-size pieces and heat them in a microwave until they turn soft.

② Mix 2 tablespoons of mayonnaise, 2 tablespoons of plain yogurt, 1 tablespoon of raisins, and a few almond slices with ①.

Pumpkin Croquette with Almond Batter

① Crush the sliced almond into coarse pieces.

② Heat 2 slices of frozen pumpkin in a microwave for about a minute. Add ½ teaspoon of kelp dashi broth (triple-concentrated type) to the pumpkin slices and roughly mash them. Then shape the mixture into a croquette.

③ Coat ② with a layer of flour, a layer of beaten egg, and a layer of ①. Deep-fry the pumpkin croquette in 356°F/180°C oil until it turns golden brown.

MUSHROOM

Japanese-Style Marinated Mushrooms

① Separate ½ pack of shimeji mushrooms and ½ pack of maitake mushrooms into small bunches. Cut 3 frozen string beans diagonally.

② Mix ①, 2 teaspoons of kelp dashi broth (triple-concentrated type), 2 teaspoons of vinegar, 1 teaspoon of sake, and ½ teaspoon of sesame oil in a heat-resistant dish.

③ Cover ② with a piece of cling wrap. Microwave it for about 2 minutes and let it rest for the flavor to settle.

CABBAGE

Cabbage and Carrot Dressed with Salted Kelp

You can find salted kelp in Japanese supermarkets, some Asian supermarkets, and online. It's usually labeled as "shio kombu." If you can't find it, you can substitute a pinch of salt or some furikake.

① Cut 1 slice of cabbage into large chunks and a small amount of carrot into thin strips.

② Place ① in a plastic bag and add a pinch of salted kelp and a small amount of sesame oil. Massage the bag and leave it until the flavor settles in.

BURDOCK ROOT

Sautéed Carrot and Burdock

① Julienne ¼ of a burdock rook and soak it in water to remove the bitterness. Julienne a small amount of carrot too.

② Heat sesame oil in a frying pan. Pat dry ① and stir-fry it.

③ Once the vegetables turns soft, pour in a small amount of sake, 1 teaspoon of soy sauce, 1 teaspoon of sugar, and 1 ½ teaspoons of mirin. Keep cooking the vegetables until the flavors blend together. Then sprinkle some ground sesame on top.

SWEET POTATO

Sweet Potato Simmered in Lemon Juice

① Cut ½ of a sweet potato into 0.4 inch/1 cm thick semicircular slices.

② Place ① in a pan and then pour water into it until the sweet potato is fully covered. Add 1 tablespoon of sugar and ½ tablespoon of lemon juice into the water and simmer it until the potato is soft.

③ Create an incision on the skin every 0.4 inch/1 cm and peel off every other piece of skin.

Candied Sweet Potato

① Cut ½ of a sweet potato into rectangular sticks and place them in water to remove the starch.

② Add 1 teaspoon of vegetable oil, 1 ½ tablespoons of sugar, ¼ teaspoon of soy sauce, and ¼ teaspoon of vinegar into a frying pan. Pat the sweet potato dry and cook it over low heat.

③ Pan-fry both sides of the sweet potato. Once the sweet potato is cooked, move it onto a plate along with the sticky sweet sauce and sprinkle some black sesame on top.

Sweet Potato and Raisin Salad
(Easy-to-cook amount)

① Peel ½ of a sweet potato. Cut it into cubes and place it in water to remove the starch.

② Soak 1 tablespoon of raisins in warm water for 10–15 minutes.

③ Boil the sweet potato from ① until it turns soft. Remove any excess water, and then mash it while it is still hot. Add in ②, 2 teaspoons of mayonnaise, and salt to taste.

Sweet Potato Croquette

① Boil a leaf-shaped snow pea in salted water.

② Boil ¼ of a sweet potato until it's soft and remove any excess water. Mix it with a small amount of salt and pepper, ½ teaspoon of butter, and 1 teaspoon of milk and then mold it into a ball.

③ Coat ② with a layer of flour, a layer of beaten egg, and a layer of panko bread crumbs. Fry the sweet potato in 356°F/180°C oil until it turns golden brown. Attach the sweet pea to the croquette with a toothpick.

POTATO

Bacon-Wrapped French Fries
(Amount for 2)

① Cut the bacon slice in half.

② Defrost 2 frozen french fries and wrap with ①.

③ Place them on a baking tray lined with aluminum foil (the wrapped end should be facing down). Roast them in a toaster oven for about 5–8 minutes.

Simmered Tri-color Veggies
(Easy-to-cook amount)

① Chop a whole potato and ½ a carrot into chunks. Place the potato in water to remove the starch. Separate ¼ of a broccoli head into smaller florets.

② Place the potato, carrots, and 1 teaspoon of powdered beef stock in a pan. Pour in enough water to cover the vegetables and bring to a boil.

③ Once the potato is soft, add the broccoli from ①. Once the broccoli is cooked, pour away the hot water and shake the pot to make the potato fluffy.

Sautéed Potato and Corn
(Easy-to-cook amount)

① Cut a small potato into quarter-circle slices. Place it in water and microwave for about 40 seconds.

② Heat vegetable oil in a frying pan and stir-fry ①, ⅛ of a carrot cut into quarter-circle slices, and 1 tablespoon of corn.

③ Once the carrot is cooked, add 1 teaspoon of butter and a small amount of soy sauce. Mix well and then add some salt and pepper to taste.

German Potato (Easy-to-cook amount)

If you cannot find a Speckkartoffeln potato from Germany, you can substitute a regular Yukon Gold potato.

① Peel one large potato. Wrap it with a wet paper towel and cling wrap and microwave it for about 4 minutes. Cut it into bite-size pieces after it's cooked.

② Cut 1 slice of bacon into thin strips and ¼ of an onion into wedges.

③ Pan-fry ② in olive oil. Once the onion is soft, add ①. When the potato has started to brown, add a small amount of powered beef stock, salt, and pepper to taste.

Potato Salad in a Cherry Tomato Cup

① Cut off the top ¼ of the cherry tomato and scoop out the bottom part with a melon baller.

② Stuff the cherry tomato with 1 teaspoon of potato salad.

BELL PEPPER

Marinated Bell Pepper and Mushroom
(Easy-to-cook amount)

① Cut the bottoms of the stems off ½ a pack of shimeji mushrooms and separate them into small bunches. Cut ¼ of red and yellow bell peppers into rectangular strips.

② Mix together ①, 2 teaspoons of olive oil, 2 teaspoons of vinegar, 1 teaspoon of sugar, ⅕ teaspoon of salt, and a pinch of granulated garlic and pepper in a heat-resistant dish.

③ Cover ② with cling wrap. Microwave it for about 2 minutes and let it rest for the flavor to settle.

CARROT

Carrots Râpées (Easy-to-cook amount)

① Julienne ½ of a carrot.

② Dice one portion of cream cheese (use the type with individually wrapped cubes).

③ Add ② to ① and mix it with 1 tablespoon of raisins, 1 teaspoon of olive oil, 1 teaspoon of honey, 1 teaspoon of lemon juice, and a little salt to taste.

Sautéed Carrot

① Julienne ¼ of a carrot.

② Heat sesame oil in a frying pan and stir-fry ①.

③ Once ② is soft, pour in a small amount of sake, 1 teaspoon of concentrated dashi broth, and a pinch of sugar. Cook until the flavors blend together and sprinkle some ground sesame on top at the end.

BROCCOLI

Marinated Broccoli and Cherry Tomato

① Boil 2 florets of broccoli in salted water. Cut 2 cherry tomatoes into quarters.

② Mix together 1 teaspoon of olive oil, 1 teaspoon of vinegar, ½ teaspoon of sugar, and a pinch of salt and pepper.

③ Pour ② on ① and marinate the vegetables for a bit.

Marinated Broccoli and Bell Pepper

Add bell pepper (seasoned with granulated garlic) to the above recipe and marinate together with broccoli.

SPINACH

Sautéed Spinach with Sakura Shrimp

① Cut a whole spinach into pieces that are 1.2 inches/3 cm long.

② Stir-fry ① in a heated frying pan with olive oil. Add 1 teaspoon of sakura shrimp and ½ teaspoon of concentrated dashi broth to taste.

LOTUS ROOT

Sautéed Lotus Root

① Cut 2 inches/5 cm of lotus root into semicircular slices and soak them in vinegar water to remove the bitterness.

② Pan-fry ① with vegetable oil.

③ Once ② is soft, pour in a small amount of sake, 1 teaspoon of concentrated dashi broth, and a pinch of bonito flakes. Cook until the flavors blend together and sprinkle some ground sesame on top at the end.

Lotus Root Dressed with Cod Roe

① Cut 1.2 inches/3 cm of lotus root into semicircular slices and boil in hot water with a small amount of vinegar.

② Mix ① with ⅛ of a mentaiko salted cod roe,* 1 teaspoon of mayonnaise, a dash of soy sauce, and some white roasted sesame seeds.

*Mentaiko can be found in Japanese and Asian supermarkets. It can be frozen or dried. This recipe uses frozen mentaiko. Please thaw mentaiko completely before usage. Cut off the needed portion and discard the membrane. If you cannot find frozen mentaiko, use a pinch of dried mentaiko or mentaiko furikake for replacement.

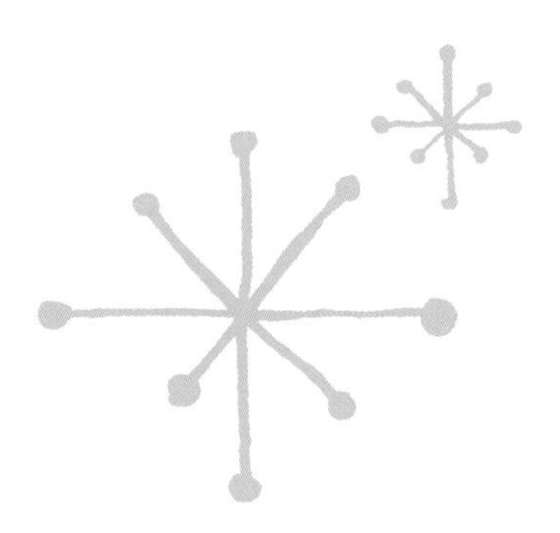

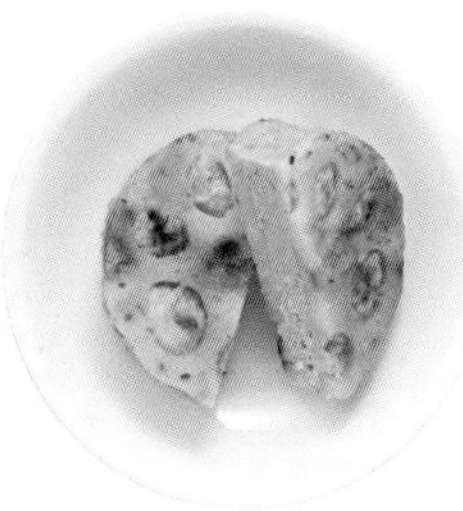

Salmon-Stuffed Lotus Root

① Remove the bones and skin from ½ slice of salmon and mince it finely with a kitchen knife. Place 2 slices of lotus root (0.2 inch/0.5 cm thick) in vinegar water.

② Mix 1 tablespoon of minced onion, 1 tablespoon of panko, 1 teaspoon of mayonnaise, a pinch of salt and pepper, and a dash of squeezed ginger juice with the salmon.

③ Pat dry the lotus root slices and coat them with a layer of potato starch. Sandwich ② in between the slices and pan-fry both sides with vegetable oil until golden brown.

Simmered Root Vegetables
(Easy-to-cook amount)

① Cut two chikuwa fish cakes into diagonal slices.

② Bring 300 ml of water, 3 tablespoons of concentrated dashi broth, 2 tablespoons of sake, and 1 tablespoon of mirin to boil. Add in ½ a pack of frozen mixed root vegetables and simmer until the flavor settles in.

Pasta

Ketchup Pasta (Easy-to-cook amount)

① Boil 3.5 oz./100 g of pasta in salted water.

② Cut 1 slice of bacon into 0.2 inch/5 mm strips. Slice ¼ of an onion and ¼ of red and yellow bell peppers.

③ Melt ½ tablespoon of butter in a frying pan and stir-fry ②. Add in 4 tablespoons of ketchup, 1 ½ tablespoons of milk, and ½ teaspoon of sugar, and bring to a boil. Add in ①. Keep tossing until the flavors are blended together and add a pinch of salt and pepper to taste.

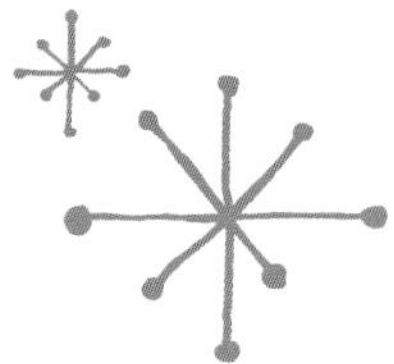

VIZ MEDIA EDITION
MASAMI MIYAZAKI

Based on the "Winnie the Pooh" works,
by A. A. Milne and E. H. Shepard.
Based on the book *The Hundred and One Dalmatians*
by Dodie Smith, published by The Viking Press.
Originally published by Boutique-sha, inc.

CREDITS – VIZ MEDIA

TRANSLATOR **Tetsuichiro Miyaki**
RECIPE TESTING **Ophelia Chien**
DESIGN **Alice Lewis**
EDITOR **Joel Enos**

Printed in Korea

Published by VIZ Media, LLC
P.O. Box 77010
San Francisco, CA 94107

10 9 8 7 6 5 4 3 2 1
First printing, July 2021

viz.com

Library of Congress Cataloging-in-Publication Data available.

CREDITS – JAPANESE STAFF

COVER / TEXT DESIGN **Chada108**
DTP **SPAIS**
PHOTOGRAPHY **Yumiko Yokota, Ryosuke Okumura (STUDIO BANBAN)**
NUTRITIONAL VALUE CALCULATION **Sayaka Mori**
PROOFREADING **Mine Kobo Co., Ltd**
EDITING **Domu Inc.**
EDITING SUPERVISION **Ryohei Maruyama**

EDITOR **Yoshiaki Fukuda**

PUBLISHER **Akira Naito**

PUBLISHER **Boutique-sha, inc.**

AUTHOR

Masami Miyazaki

Masami Miyazaki is a teacher and blogger who started creating character bento when her son, a picky eater, entered kindergarten. Her award-winning bento and recipe work has been featured in numerous magazines and recipe books in Japan.

BLOG: JURU'S CHARACTER BENTO

http://juru.at.webry.info/